Mary Henderson's
PARIS EMBASSY COOKBOOK

HÔTEL DE L'AMBASSADEUR D'ANGLETERRE.

The Residence of the British Ambassador, rue du Faubourg St Honoré

Mary Henderson's PARIS EMBASSY COOKBOOK

200 distinctive Anglo-French recipes

Weidenfeld and Nicolson · London

For Alexandra, my daughter, who loves cooking as
much as I do, and for Patrick, son of Monsieur Viaëne,
who is likewise following in his father's footsteps:
may both of them enjoy cooking *à la Franglaise.*

The publishers wish to thank the following for
permission to reproduce copyright photographs: Bibliothèque
Nationale, Paris (pages 22, 42, 60, 94, 108, 118, 132, 170
and 188); Chatsworth House (page 10); Derry Moore (page 12)

First Published in Great Britain in 1980 by
George Weidenfeld and Nicolson Ltd, 91 Clapham High Street, London SW4

Line drawings by the author

ISBN 0 297 77647 9

Printed in Great Britain by
Fakenham Press Limited
Fakenham, Norfolk

CONTENTS

INTRODUCTION

Good English cooking is delicious; good French cuisine is still, today, the very best. So what a delight for me, a keen amateur cook, to have the opportunity to combine the two in the British Embassy in Paris, a beautiful house which historically unites Anglo-French taste. What fun to see Nanny's Guard's Pudding served up to French Ministers on the Wellington silver, or Alsatian Quail Pie served to the Queen Mother at a table decorated with the famous silver gilt centrepiece by Thomire (1751–1843), a gift to the Embassy from George IV. (Originally, Napoleon commissioned these as gifts for members of his family. George IV therefore made a very appropriate present to the British Embassy.)

The eighteenth-century Hôtel de Charost, which is now the Paris Embassy, was built in 1720 from plans by Louis XV's architect and engineer, Mazin. It was commissioned by Arman de Béthune, Duc de Charost (great-grandson of Fouquet) and was built alongside fifteen other elegant *Hôtels* which housed the aristocracy of the day on the Grande rue du Faubourg St Honoré. The design, which has barely changed today, was typical of that period *'entre cour et jardin'*. On the street side, two pavilions and a large porch or *porte cochère* opened on to a semi-circular courtyard. This was flanked on either side by arcades (one has now been removed, and the other filled in for the kitchens). The stables were housed in one pavilion, indicated by two carved horses' heads over the entrance; the kitchens were in the other, with a carved wild boar and hound over the doorway. The grand reception rooms were on the garden side of the building.

In 1803 Maria-Paola Bonaparte (later Princess Pauline Borghese), the twenty-two-year-old widow of General Leclerc, bought the Hôtel from the heirs of the Duc de Charost. 'Paoletta' – as her family and friends called her – was Napoleon's favourite sister and he paid the major part of the purchase price. Over a period of eleven years – on and off, it is true, as Pauline travelled a good deal and later Napoleon gave her the *château* of Neuilly – the Hôtel de Charost, or the *Nid de Pauline*, as it was known at that time, was the elegant and

Central portion of the *surtout de table* designed by Thomire

luxurious centre of the *nouvelle vague*, the centre and epitome of flamboyant Empire taste.

Pauline enlarged and redecorated her home, borrowing money from her brother and sister Elisa in order to do so. She brought in the best architects, Percier and Fontaine, and ordered furniture from the best cabinet-makers, the Jacob brothers. She added sphynxes and garlands to the eighteenth-century decorations, and hung the walls with silk and tassels from Lyon. Her gilt *'lit de parade'* (a bed for lying in state) was crowned with ostrich feathers and a hovering golden Napoleonic eagle. For her balls and receptions she enlarged the house on the garden side. One wing she used as her State dining room, to seat sixty-three (sixty guests, the Emperor, Josephine and Pauline). It was lit by two giant chandeliers, each with sixteen candles set in the heads of gilt zephyrs. Scattered on the floor were thirty imitation leopard-skin rugs. The other wing housed the Borghese collection of paintings.

Although Pauline's critics have said that she dressed solely with the idea of undressing, the Princess had style and always dressed in the height of Empire fashion – deepest *décolleté*, high waist and transparent flowing muslin. This last was bought by the famous couturier Le Roy in contraband from England during the blockade. Napoleon no doubt was not informed of this cross-Channel transaction.

Pauline was frivolous – it was said of her that 'she danced throughout the winter, took baths throughout the summer and loved all the year round' – but she was extremely devoted and loyal to her brother. After the first Abdication (4 April 1814), she gave orders to sell her Paris home so that she could follow Napoleon to Elba. There was considerable haggling over the final price and this resulted in the sale including all the valuable fittings, chandeliers, clocks and furniture. The Duke of Wellington, acting on the Prince Regent's behalf, finally signed the inventory and bought the Hôtel in August that year. Until then, British Ambassadors in Paris had rented houses; now Wellington, and all his successors, would have a permanent Embassy.

Wellington remained in Paris as Ambassador for only four months but he, like many who followed him, entertained with brilliance, ease and elegance in the gilt salons of the former Hôtel de Charost. Ambassadors who have succeeded him have had their problems, some political, others financial. In 1835,

Pauline Borghese by Robert Lefèvre (oil on canvas)

for instance, Palmerston refused to sanction the cost of repairs and wanted to sell the Embassy. Some Ambassadresses have disliked the social whirl of diplomatic life – one of my early predecessors, Lady Tyrell, retired up a tree in the garden to write a history of the world. Other Ambassadresses have been somewhat eccentric, like Lady Clerk. A faith-healer and painter, she gave Chagall a room on the second floor of the Residence and once forced her guests to play musical chairs instead of listening to a concert her husband had arranged. (As one of her French guests left the Residence that night, bruised after missing her chair, she was heard to remark that she preferred conversation to English games.) And then there was the *gamine* daughter of Lord Harding, who ordered bread to be baked in the shape of frogs for a dinner party.

There have of course been memorable balls and receptions; the Hôtel provides an ideal setting for these. In 1826 there was

Lady Granville

a grand New Year's ball given by Lord Granville for some 1,150 guests. The following day Lady Granville wrote: 'I cannot make my accounts come right.' And there was the masked ball given by Lord Stuart de Rothesay in 1829 when his wife appeared dramatically at the top of the grand staircase dressed as Mary Queen of Scots. Just after the war Lady Diana Cooper's 'salon', which she held in the Salon Vert, was a memorable gathering of politicians, writers, artists and decorators.

Today, although the Hôtel is very much as it was in Pauline Borghese's time, we do not give balls every Wednesday or concerts every Saturday as she did. And Nicko, my husband, does not ride down the Champs Elysées as Wellington did: he does however walk his dog there. But we try to keep up the tradition of the house – making our French and British guests at home in a French house which has an English atmosphere. Roses fill the Wellington silver soup tureens. The gilt mirrors in the salons reflect the English garden, a work of love by former Ambassadors and Ambassadresses. The walls are hung with valuable pictures donated or loaned by British patrons and galleries. Finally our table, which moves from salon to salon in the eighteenth-century manner (I try to avoid the State dining room), serves an international cuisine with a British and French flavour.

The French today, as in the past, mind about food and they take Talleyrand's advice seriously – '*Les bons diners font la bonne diplomatie*'. The President, Monsieur Giscard d'Estaing, chooses his official menus personally; the Prime Minister, Monsieur Barre, is a first-class cook himself and even draws on culinary metaphors in his speeches to rub home a political argument. ('The economic situation', he has said, 'is like a mayonnaise which at a certain moment needs just a drop of oil to set.') If, then, the flattering and kind guests and friends we have entertained feel that the British are no longer what the French nineteenth-century caricaturists described as '*Des monstrueux insulaires devorant des boeufs rotis*' (insular monsters devouring roast bulls), '*des gloutons tourant la broche arrosant de jus des pommes de terre bouilles*' (gluttons turning the spit, watering their boiled potatoes with gravy), I think I have succeeded in my task and for this I am grateful to the gifted French chef Monsieur Viaëne, his *sous-chef* Alain Druard, *pâtissier* Gérard Delafoy, and *commis* Eric Lasserre.

The chef and his team. From Left to right, Gérard, M. Viaëne, Alain and Eric

THE CHEF

The chef, Monsieur James Viaëne, is of Flemish origin; his grandfather was Belgian. He is tall, fair and gentle to the point of shyness. He is unflappable and a master of organization. Whether he is preparing a dinner for fifty or a buffet for two hundred and fifty the kitchens remain spotless; the copper pans glisten, the pastry boards are dusted with flour as if touched by a light frost; balloon whisks, sieves, strainers and spatulas are used, washed and put back in place with clockwork precision. An atmosphere of concentration and creation reigns. Alain, the *sous-chef* (the undercook), prepares one dish, Gérard, the *patissier* (the pastry cook), prepares another, Eric, the *commis* (the kitchen boy) helps everyone, and the chef supervises his team – giving a word of advice here, a helping hand there – before applying himself to the form and finish of everything before it is served.

Born on 11 August 1937 at Crépy-en-Valois (Oise), north of Paris, Viaëne was brought up the hard way during the war and post-war years. He needed little to make him happy as a child – his favourite toys were a set of tiny cake tins which he would fill and 'bake'. Such was his passion for cakes that at the age of fourteen he asked his parents to allow him to work in Senlis in Monsieur Chaumard's noted pastry shop. To this day Viaëne recalls how his first master was stern but 'had a heart of gold' and how he insisted on 'quality rather than quantity' – a maxim the young apprentice was to follow throughout his career.

In 1954 Viaëne took the first step in his Anglo-French career when he went to work in London for Ambassador René Massigli. In the splendid French Embassy in Kensington he was the *plongeur*: he washed up plates and peeled vegetables, but at the same time managed to keep an eagle eye on the talented chef, Monsieur Gonin. When Monsieur Massigli left London, the young kitchen boy returned to France and entered the Duchess of Windsor's service. Once again Viaëne worked close to first-class chefs, first Monsieur Legro and then Monsieur Massy. Excellence, care and attention to detail were the orders in the Windsor household and the style set by the Duchess and the perfection of her Parisian receptions have left their mark.

Viaëne stayed four years with the Duchess of Windsor, left to do his military service and then returned for a further six months before striking out to become a master himself. He worked as an assistant to the gifted Monsieur Harmand, a chef famous for the highly original dishes he served for the art historian and Member of the Academy, Monsieur Daniel Wildenstein, and Madame Wildenstein. Two years later Viaëne was ready to be on his own. He served Monsieur and Madame Joao de Souza Lange in their English-style house, 'Wood Lodge', near Chantilly for four years, then worked for Monsieur and Madame Michel David Weill of Lazards in Paris for a further four years. It was in these two fine houses that he was able to turn his apprenticeship to full use and for the first time create his own cuisine.

It is now eight years since Viaëne became the treasured chef at the British Embassy under Sir Christopher (now Lord) Soames and Lady Soames. Like others who followed them, the Soames, who entertained with panache, greatly appreciated Viaëne's qualities, and it is said that Sir Christopher had tears in his eyes when he shook the chef's hand on leaving the Embassy.

Viaëne is a dedicated chef whose work gives him great satisfaction. He says that one of his happiest memories is of the

A ball at the Embassy in 1856

time when he was making a replica in sugar of Queen Elizabeth's crown for our Silver Jubilee party. Working from the official portrait we have in the Embassy and a coloured print, he meticulously copied every jewel. He started work in the morning and went on throughout the night, losing all sense of time and place. Apart from his own genius as a chef, I have noticed another exceptional quality – his talent for teaching others. His twenty-seventh kitchen boy has just entered our service at the Embassy. His earlier apprentices have become chefs and assistant chefs in famous restaurants or in Paris's most noted households, including the Elysée. Viaëne has never forced his apprentices to choose cooking as a career; in fact he has often advised those whom he thought were not born to be chefs to do something else. One former kitchen boy is now happily chopping wood and helping his father in the forest – he preferred an outdoor life; others have become butlers or *maîtres d'hôtel*, being more suited to that aspect of catering. Today, rather like Proust's Madame de Caillevet, Monsieur Viaëne holds a 'salon' – and you can really call it that – in the Embassy kitchens. His seconds or apprentices and their friends drop in and gather round to discuss, amend, adapt and learn more about cuisine. They are always welcome, as is anyone as passionately devoted to the art of cooking as is Viaëne.

THE TEAM

Alain Druard, born in Paris in 1956, is our *sous-chef*. Alain started cooking, he says, because he 'loved eating'. He is a gifted, attractive boy and stands in extremely well for his master on the chef's days off. He loves the detail that goes into the dishes we serve and can spend hours (the chef says, rather sternly, rather too many hours) placing the thinnest cucumber scales on cold poached salmon for buffets – to the delight of our guests who rave over the beauty of the dish. Alain wants to go to the United States and then return to France to open a restaurant where he can serve what he calls *'la cuisine raffinée'* – which he has learned from the chef.

Our *patissier* is Gérard Delafoy. Born in the Vendée (the west coast of France) in 1957, he started reading cookery books at an early age and is now an excellent pastry cook. He loves helping the chef to make the intricate and decorative sweets which must, of course, always be done at the last minute. He enjoys baking English cakes and puddings and wants to make pastry cooking his career.

Eric Lasserre was born in Bordeaux in 1958. As a child he loved helping his mother in the kitchen. Today he is our *commis* – the position his master held years ago in the French Embassy in London. He is interested in the Anglo-French cuisine that he has learned at the Embassy and, like the chef, he has a particular bent for pastry cooking. One day he, too, wants to have his own restaurant, preferably in the Landes, the southwest coast where some of his favourite dishes come from – such as *La lamproie à la bordelaise*. (The lamprey is bled, cooked in red wine, tossed with slices of leeks and bacon and served with a sauce to which the blood is added.)

ENTERTAINING

Official entertaining has kept its traditional style in Paris. White-gloved waiters in livery stand behind gilt chairs, soft music plays at official banquets, crystal chandeliers glitter and reflect their lights in the golden mirrors. For the guests the two most important elements of a *Soirée officielle* have remained as in the past – where they sit and what they eat. *Préséance à table*, seating plans, are still almost a matter of life and death, with protocol departments of the Elysée and the Quai (the President's office and the Foreign Office) working overtime as harassed secretaries and hostesses ring for advice. And, of course, the choice of food is of paramount importance.

The Elysée sets the pattern of elegance. Every day the President chooses his menus from suggestions made by his chef, Monsieur Le Serub, and handed to him by his comptroller. He likes to try out new dishes such as *Foie d'oie chaud aux pommes Calville* (hot goose liver with a sweet cottage apple called Calville) and often includes his favourite dessert, *Chocolat Forêt Noire* (a delicious chocolate cake with cherries). Such is the importance of the President's official table that it travels with him, so to speak, on state visits. For example, his chef, the kitchen staff, the food, the kitchen equipment, hot plates and all, together with the priceless Sèvres dinner service and the Elysée silver – some two plane-loads – were once flown to Brazil for a three-day visit.

At the Matignon (partly built by the eighteenth-century architect, Mazin), the Prime Minister, Monsieur Barre, entertains with warmth and style. When alone he likes to cook his favourite dish, *Poulet Bonne Femme* (a chicken *flambé* with cognac and gently simmered with spring onions, peas and tiny carrots), but when entertaining officially Madame Barre arranges her guests at round tables with a beautiful bunch of flowers on each table – each bunch a different colour. Guests have their colour marked on their place card so that they can find their table. Madame Barre chooses her menus carefully, and along with French specialities she includes dishes from Italy and her native Hungary. To please her husband, who was born in Réunion, she serves spiced dishes – the Prime Minister particularly likes fish and chicken with a saffron and ginger sauce which he finds 'has a more refined taste than curry'.

The design of menu cards for official parties in Paris today is taken extremely seriously. The President of France personally chooses rare prints from the Louvre's *Cabinet d'Estampes* or from other museums. For the state dinner he offered H.M. Queen Elizabeth in the French Embassy in London on 24 June 1976, he chose a bunch of anemones by Nicolas Robert (1614–85). (Madame Giscard's christian name is Anne-Aymone.) For the lunch he offered H.M. Queen Elizabeth the Queen Mother in Paris at the Elysée on 28 October 1976, he

Queen Victoria's visit to the
Embassy, August 1868

chose a Fragonard drawing. The Prime Minister, the Foreign
Minister and other French ministers have menus decorated
with a print of the *Place* or *Hôtel* of their official residence. The
diplomatic corps in Paris follow the tradition, too, and take
great trouble over their menu cards. The US Embassy has an
original touch – it combines place cards with the menu. The
folded place card when unfolded has the menu written on it.
The German Embassy prints the guest's name on the menu
just below a drawing of the Embassy – Prince Eugène de
Beauharnais's former palace.

One cannot talk of entertaining in a grand style without
mentioning the Rothschilds. Here it is amusing to note that at
the Hôtel Lambert the fabulous wines Baron Guy de
Rothschild serves are not put on the menu; they are whispered
in your ear by the *sommelier*, as in the olden days. However, at
dinner at Mouton or Lafite in the Médoc the menu lists all the
wines; sometimes for a grand occasion there are as many as
five. Finally it is worth noting that at Latour – that famous
British-owned château – the menu gives only the wines; the
food is just there as an accompaniment. We at the British

Embassy have a tradition of writing out the menus and place cards by hand; these are written by my social secretary, Frances Howarth. Our guests always comment on her handwriting and take the menus away with them. One guest asked to see the 'scribe we hide in the attic'.

The real revolution in entertaining is an invitation which is now the rage in Paris – a card inviting you to a '*cocktail-dîner*' or '*prendre un verre*', to drop in for a drink and leave or stay to supper. It is a kind of *cocktail prolongé* – except that there are no cocktails, just champagne and red wine. There is a simple buffet which often includes scrambled eggs cooked with smoked salmon (*chez* the Comtesse Hubert d'Ornano) or *cassoulet* (*chez* the Baronne Alain de Rothschild) or cheese puffs and herrings with a special sour cream sauce and black bread (*chez* la Marquise de Ganay). This is usually followed by cheese, a tart, ice cream and fruit salad. Guests help themselves and either sit at round tables – unplaced! – or try to balance a plate on their knees. It is all very *décontracté*, very relaxed, and is very popular.

We at the Embassy have followed the fashion, too. Of course we are expected to entertain formally, and we do, but we also give many buffet parties with round tables and a choice of food on the buffet. We find this is the best way for our guests to move around and have the chance of talking to more people – and to choose their favourite dish from the buffet.

Every Monday the chef and I go through our plans for the week. We discuss new dishes and correct previous recipes which we think were not quite right. We discuss the guests and decide on the menus. Giovanni Fiore, the butler, is present so that he can let my husband know what dishes we are serving when he chooses the wines from the cellar. Each menu is very carefully thought out, whether it is for a small official lunch, a state dinner or the Jubilee ball. The chef and I try to serve French guests with something English and English guests with something French, but we also like to include our favourite international recipes. We always serve British cheeses to our French guests – Stilton and mature Cheddar – and French cheeses to our British guests.

Guests may find that they are given the same dish twice. We do keep lists of our guests (last year some two thousand guests came to lunches and dinners at the Embassy) with the menus we have served them, but we think that if there is a particularly

Oeufs écossais de cailles au nid
Taramosalata

Pie de gibier en croute
Chou rouge - Riz à l'indienne
Salade
Stilton - Cheddar
Panier de lychees
Sauce gingembre - Brandy snaps
Château Fuissé 1971
Gevrey Chambertin Clos Prieur 1969
Château Guiraud 1970
dîner du   17 octobre

A menu written by Frances
Howarth

successful dish it should be repeated as a *spécialité de la maison*.

Our recipes may sometimes be complicated, and their preparation needs time, love and care. Writing out some of the chef's recipes I have often been tempted to add: 'I do this in the liquidizer, and I leave this out ...' but then I remember the enthusiastic exclamations provoked by the arrival of one of the chef's original creations. How often some awkward meeting or some sticky political situation has been eased by the beautifully cooked and beautifully presented dishes the chef has prepared. It is for this reason that I have collected our most successful recipes. They are, I hope, an important record of the elegance of French cuisine in Paris today and of its union with British cuisine. This culinary marriage is a happy one; it suffers none of the ups and downs of the age-long Anglo-French political love affair. Each dish mentioned in the book, whether French, British or international in flavour has been adapted in an Anglo-French style. If the recipes seem complicated, try some of the easy ones first to give you confidence. The suggestions are as good for six as for sixty or a hundred. Choose one or two of them and adapt them to suit yourself. You will find that they all have a certain flavour, a certain look – a flavour of France and a taste of Britain and that little extra something that only a French chef can add. Happy cooking and *bon appétit*.

MARY HENDERSON
Paris, November 1978

Notes et Mesures
General Notes and Measures

LE BEURRE (BUTTER)
French butter is used throughout the book. It is fresh unsalted butter.

LA CRÈME (CREAM)
French cream is used in this book which is a matured cream unlike English cream. English double cream is the nearest equivalent and in the US American whipping cream can be used.

LE POIVRE ET LES FINES HERBES (PEPPER AND HERBS)
The chef uses black pepper for most of his dishes. He uses white pepper for dishes where the black pepper would colour the sauce or dish. (For example a white béchamel, a white fish, etc.) He uses pepper and herbs sparingly, reminding his under-chefs that too many different flavours spoil a dish.

LES MESURES (MEASURES)
Converting French measures into the English equivalent is always a problem. You will find that conversions in the recipes vary, sometimes taking 25 g to be one ounce, more often 30 g as one ounce. For convenience, 500 g is usually converted to 1 lb except in cases such as pastry, where measurements must be more precise. Liquid measures similarly range from 500 ml = 1 pint to 600 ml = 1 pint (the actual conversion is 560 ml). When liquid measures are expressed as ounces, it refers to weight. For small quantities the following approximate measures have been used:

butter	1 dessertspoon ($\frac{1}{2}$ oz)	= 15 g
liquids	1 dessertspoon	= 15 ml
sugar	1 dessertspoon ($\frac{3}{4}$ oz)	= 20–25 g
salt	1 teaspoon ($\frac{1}{5}$ oz)	= 6 g

An English cup is not the same size as an American cup and a French cup depends on whose cup it is. If you use the same cup throughout the recipes you should not have any trouble. The same rule applies for spoons, which differ from country to country and from house to house.

SIEVES AND STRAINERS

When I first arrived in Paris the chef gave me a list of equipment he needed. Most of it was what I, as a cook myself, could well believe he needed. But the number of sieves, all different sizes and meshes, and the number of strainers of different shapes and sizes amazed me. Now, however, I realize what an important part these play in French cuisine. Throughout the book there are items pressed through sieves, poured through strainers – even after they have been liquidized. If you are cooking in a small kitchen and for a few friends you may well hesitate to follow each of the chef's steps in the recipes. But for those who have time and help in the kitchen I have noted the exact method used, because the results have always been so excellent and so appreciated by our guests.

L'ARRIVÉE.

Un Anglais attaqué du Spleen, vient se faire traiter en France.

An Englishman suffering from an 'attack of spleen' comes to be treated in France . . .

ENTRÉES

Welsh Rarebit Artichokes	Fonds d'Artichauts Welsh Rarebit
Eggs in Purses	Œufs en Bourses
Scrambled Eggs à la Portugaise	Œufs Brouillés à la Portugaise
Eggs Vert-Pré in Flower	Œufs Vert-Pré en Fleur
Nest of Scotch Quail Eggs	Œufs Écossais de Cailles au Nid
Quiche Lorraine Sophie	Quiche Lorraine Sophie
Greek Stuffed Courgettes	Courgettes Farcies à la Grecque
The Chef's Pheasant Pâté	Pâté de Faisan du Chef
Barcelona Spinach Tart	Tarte Barcelona
Leek Tart	Tarte aux Poireaux
Poached Egg Soufflé	Soufflé aux Œufs Pochés
Four Cheese Mousse	Mousse aux Quatre Fromages
Scotch Eggs	Œufs Écossais
Iced Cucumber Soup	Soup de Concombre Glacée
Gazpacho	Gazpacho
Russian Bortsch with Pirojkis	Bortsch Russe avec Pirojkis
Polish Barszcz	Barszcz Polonais
Greek Avgolemono Consommé	Consommé Grecque Avgolemono
Saint Germain Soup	Potage Saint Germain

Fonds d'Artichauts Welsh Rarebit
Welsh Rarebit Artichokes

Serving Welsh rarebit on toast to a number of guests is impossible – the toast becomes soggy and it never really works. This is why I adapted the recipe so that the Welsh rarebit mixture is served on artichoke hearts. The result is an original Anglo-French dish which is an excellent starter or entrée.

SERVES 6

12 artichokes
3 lemons
1 bowl of cold water containing
   the juice of 2 lemons
consommé or stock (page 174)

1 sharp kitchen knife
1 pair kitchen scissors
1 large saucepan

Break the stalks off at the base of the artichokes and cut and trim the base of the hearts, preferably with a stainless steel knife. Cut off the leaves (with kitchen scissors or a sharp knife) down to the heart, leaving the hairy chokes. Squeeze the juice of 3 lemons over the hearts and rub them well with the juice to prevent them turning black. Do one at a time and then drop them into a bowl of cold water containing the juice of the other 2 lemons. Stir from time to time, then drain the hearts and cook them in a pan of boiling consommé. You will need just enough consommé to cover the artichokes, about 1 litre (2 pints). Cooking time depends on the quality of the artichokes but cook them until the hairy choke is easily removed. Drain, remove choke with a small spoon and place hearts in a greased baking dish.

For the Welsh Rarebit:
250 g (9 oz) Cheddar or Cheshire
   cheese, grated
20 g (⅔ oz) butter
100 ml (⅙ pint) milk or ale
½ teaspoon mustard
½ teaspoon cayenne pepper or
   paprika
salt
Worcestershire sauce

1 small heavy-bottomed pan

Welsh Rarebit, Fondue de Fromage:
Dissolve the cheese and the butter in the milk or beer in a small heavy-bottomed pan, over a gentle heat. Then add the mustard, pepper, a pinch of salt and a dash of Worcestershire sauce.

   Spoon this Welsh rarebit mixture on to the centre of the artichoke hearts. Scatter a little cayenne pepper or paprika over them and cook in a very hot oven, 240 °C (475 °F)/Mark 9, for 15 minutes. Serve immediately.

   Our chef decorates his baking dish by scattering very finely chopped fresh parsley all over it and laying the artichokes over this.

Œufs en Bourses
Eggs in Purses

This is an original dish. It requires twelve thin pancakes (without any holes in them), twelve poached eggs and a sauce choron. *My chef and I had fun making this the* entrée *for a lunch given at the Embassy for the former Chancellor of the Exchequer, Denis Healey, and the Governor of the Bank of England, Gordon Richardson.*

SERVES 6

For the pancakes:
125 g (4 oz) flour
2 eggs
200 ml (⅓ pint) milk
pinch salt
30 g (1 oz) melted butter

1 mixing bowl
1 fine strainer

For the eggs:
12 eggs
vinegar
salt

1 large pan

For the purses:
sauce choron (page 121)
oil for deep frying

string
1 deep frying pan

Place the flour in a bowl, add 2 eggs, the cold milk and a pinch of salt. Mix well and put through a fine strainer. The batter should be light and clear. Add the melted butter and allow the mixture to stand for 3 hours. The pancakes can be prepared in advance.

To poach the 12 eggs, have a pan of boiling water ready, and add some vinegar (about 2 dessertspoons to 1 litre (2 pints) water). Break the eggs one at a time into a cup and slide them gently into the boiling water. Allow them to boil for 3 minutes. The white film must be just solid enough to cover the yolk as the poached egg is, in fact, just a boiled egg without a shell.

Plunge them into cold water, trim them if necessary and keep them ready in a bowl of cold salted water – about 7 g (1 teaspoon) salt per litre (2 pints) water – until needed. The success of a poached egg depends on its freshness – the fresher it is the lighter and better the poached egg.

Make the purses by spreading a teaspoon of *sauce choron* in the centre of each of the pancakes, then place a poached egg on top and close the pancakes with a little string, drawing up the edges to enclose the egg. Repeat this for 12 eggs. Have a deep frying pan of boiling vegetable oil ready. Plunge the eggs into this for about 2 minutes, drain, cut the string and serve the little purses upright with the remains of the sauce handed round separately. This dish should be served as soon as possible so that the yolks remain soft.

Œufs Brouillés à la Portugaise
Scrambled Eggs à la Portugaise

I must confess that for this dish, and for many others, my chef and I have allowed for two servings per person as the cassolettes *are so light and delicious that we find that most guests have a second helping. The dish really requires the classic French* fer à cassolettes *which can be obtained quite easily in France. If you cannot find one you can compromise and use some light tart shells. The* fer *is like a fluted deep tartlette mould with a handle. If you wanted to make one you could solder a handle on to a tartlette mould.*

SERVES 6
For the cassolettes:
200 ml (⅓ pint) milk
4 egg whites
1 dessertspoon oil
pinch salt
125 g (4 oz) flour
oil for deep frying

1 mixing bowl
1 fine strainer
1 saucepan for deep frying
fondue de tomate Portugaise (page 126)

For the eggs:
1 dessertspoon butter
8 eggs
3 dessertspoons fresh cream
salt and pepper

1 saucepan
1 double boiler
1 egg whisk

2 dessertspoons parsley or green peppers, finely chopped

Mix the milk, egg whites, oil and salt into the flour. This should give you a light, fairly liquid pancake batter. Put it through a fine strainer. Heat the oil (we use peanut oil) and when it is very hot, dip the *fer à cassolettes* into the oil, drain, and dip into the batter. (Allow the batter to coat about three-quarters of the outside of the *fer*, leaving a rim around the top of the mould.) Carefully dip the *fer* again into the hot frying oil and cook until the batter is a light golden colour. Then give the *fer* a firm rap to detach the shell (you can use a wooden spatula for this), allow the shell to drop into the frying oil and cook until the inner part is golden – about 15 seconds. Remove and keep warm, while you make the remaining 11 shells.

Prepare a *fondue de tomate Portugaise*.

To scramble the eggs, dissolve the butter in a saucepan, break the eggs into it and add the cream, salt and pepper. Place the saucepan in a double boiler with boiling water and beat the mixture with an egg whisk or a wooden spoon. The eggs must be wet and light; if by any chance they are dry, add another yolk or a little cream. I must admit that these scrambled eggs *à la Française* are delicious and bear little resemblance to what one is sometimes served for breakfast.

To serve:
Line the 12 *cassolettes* with the *fondue de tomate Portugaise* (about ½ dessertspoon per shell), fill with scrambled eggs, decorate with finely-chopped parsley or green peppers and serve immediately.

Œufs Vert-Pré en Fleur
Eggs Vert-Pré in Flower

This dish was invented by my chef and me – it is an adaptation of the traditional œufs vert pré, which are œufs mollets served in small pastry boats. Instead we serve them on artichoke hearts and they come in looking like exotic green flowers. It is easy to prepare in advance. It requires artichokes, eggs mollet, a mirepoix and a sauce verte.

SERVES 6

6 artichokes
2 lemons
salt

1 sharp knife
1 large saucepan
1 pair kitchen scissors

For the œufs mollets:
6 eggs

2 saucepans

For the mirepoix (optional):
120 g (4 oz) carrots, diced
120 g (4 oz) onions, diced
1 shallot, finely chopped
2 parsley stalks, finely chopped
8 tarragon leaves, finely chopped
1 dessertspoon butter

1 small heavy-bottomed pan
with lid

The artichokes must be fresh and tender. Break off the stems right up near to the base of the heart. Wash the artichokes and trim the rounded base with a sharp knife. Rub them with lemon (this stops them turning black), then cook in plenty of boiling salted water. After about 15–20 minutes, test to see if they are ready – that is, if the centre leaves come out easily. Take them out and plunge them into cold water. Drain, remove most of the leaves and the hairy chokes, leaving a rim of 8 or 9 leaves on each, which should be trimmed into points to look like flower petals. Do this with scissors.

Œufs mollets:
Cook the eggs in a pan of boiling water for 6 minutes (from the time the water boils after the eggs have been put in). Then plunge them into cold water and remove the shells. Keep the eggs in cold salted water until needed, then drain.

Mirepoix:
Make the *mirepoix* by sweating the carrots, onions, shallot and herbs in the butter for 10 minutes in a small covered pan. Pour off the butter and allow the mixture to cool.

Prepare a *sauce verte* or green sauce (page 128) and serve the finished dish as follows: place a little *mirepoix* in each of the artichoke hearts, put an egg on top and cover with some *sauce verte*. As a special decoration, one watercress leaf looks beautiful, and the whole can be served on a bed of chopped parsley. Our colour-conscious chef adds radishes, cut open like flowers, between the artichokes and sometimes cuts the watercress leaf carefully into the shape of a heart and a diamond and places these on each coated egg.

Note: The *mirepoix* is optional. The chef includes it when he is cooking for a small lunch or dinner.

Œufs Écossais de Cailles au Nid
Nest of Scotch Quail Eggs

I taught my chef how to make Scotch eggs and we serve them with great success at large buffets. Cut in half they decorate the cold meat dishes and in France they are an original British touch. But true to the traditions of French cuisine, my chef suggested doing the same thing to quail eggs – I had of course never thought of such finesse and to add an amusing touch I suggested we served them as an entrée in little potato nests. Here is the recipe which is very pretty.

SERVES 6

18 quail eggs
85 g (3 oz) flour, sieved
540 g (1 lb 2 oz) sausagemeat, very finely minced
2 eggs
salt and pepper
2 teaspoons olive oil
115 g (4 oz) fresh breadcrumbs
2 litres (3½ pints) oil for frying

1 bowl of cold water
1 sieve
1 mixing bowl
1 deep frying pan

For the nests:
6 large potatoes, very finely shredded
2 litres (3½ pints) oil for frying
chopped parsley

2 wire mesh ladles, one smaller than the other
1 deep frying pan

Boil the quail eggs for 5 minutes, shell and allow them to cool in a bowl of cold water. When they are cold, roll them in the sifted flour. Moisten your hands in cold water and flatten about 30 g (1 oz) of the sausagemeat.

Place an egg in the middle and press the sausagemeat round it so that the egg is encased. Repeat this process for all the eggs, then roll them again in the flour. Beat the 2 standard eggs with salt and pepper and the olive oil. Roll each coated egg in the beaten egg and then in the breadcrumbs. Take great care that each egg is carefully rolled in all these ingredients. Finally, heat the frying oil (we use peanut oil) and deep fry the eggs for 3 minutes. Drain and allow them to get cold.

Nests:
Carefully wash and dry the shredded potatoes. Take the two wire mesh ladles, one smaller than the other, and dip them into the deep frying oil. Then press the potatoes into the bigger ladle and place the smaller one on top. Fry in the oil at about 190 °C (375 °F) until very dry. Unmould and allow to cool. Repeat until you have made 6 nests. When the nests are cold place them on a bed of chopped parsley, cut the eggs in halves and place them in the nests.

We serve a *sauce tartar* with this dish. My chef's tartar sauce is a Rémoulade sauce to which he adds chopped egg yolks (page 128). We have served Greek tarama sauce with the dish (page 58) and it was a great success.

Quiche Lorraine Sophie

This is a recipe my mother used and I like it because it is unlike the usual quiche. It looks like a beautiful cheese soufflé tart – taller than the traditional quiche. You can use either shrimps or the more usual bacon and ham, if you wish. You can of course use mushrooms too; this is a matter of personal taste. This quiche takes longer to cook than the traditional ones and should be allowed to stand for a while before cutting. It then cuts neatly into slices like a cake. If you find that your guests are late you can leave the quiche (un-cut) in a low oven with foil paper over it and nothing goes wrong.

SERVES 8

400 g (14 oz) shortcrust pastry
  (page 178)
100 g (3½ oz) each lean ham and
  lean bacon, diced, or 600 g
  (1 lb 5 oz) shrimps, shelled
40 g (1½ oz) butter

1 25-cm (10-in) cake tin, greased
greaseproof paper
dry white baking beans
1 frying pan

For fondue:
400 ml (14 oz) fresh cream
80 g (2½ oz) butter
40 g (1½ oz) cornflour
250 g (9 oz) Gruyère or Cheddar
  cheese, grated
freshly-ground black pepper
1 teaspoon fresh mustard
6–7 eggs, separated

1 medium-sized heavy-bottomed
  pan
1 wire whisk
foil paper

Line the cake tin, allowing the pastry to reach about three-quarters of the way up the sides. Prick the base and cover with a circle of greaseproof paper and beans to stop the pastry from rising. Cook in a moderate oven, 200 °C (400 °F)/Mark 6, for 15 minutes, then remove the paper and beans and let the pastry dry out in the oven with door open for 5 minutes. Lightly fry the ham and bacon, or the shrimps, in butter, then scatter them on the bottom of the tart (keep some back for decoration) and dot with butter.

Heat the cream and keep it warm while you heat the butter, add the cornflour and stir. Pour in the heated cream all at once and beat with a wire whisk. Remove from fire and add the grated cheese, black pepper and mustard. Stir and return to the fire, stirring with a whisk until the mixture is just on the boil. Remove and beat in the egg yolks one at a time. Allow the mixture to cool, then fold in the beaten egg whites. Mix well. Pour into the tart, scatter a little of the bacon etc. on the top, cover with foil paper and place in a preheated hot oven, 220 °C (425 °F)/Mark 7, for 10 minutes, then lower to 200 °C (400 °F)/Mark 6 for 25 minutes. Test the centre with a knife to see if the quiche is cooked. If the mixture still sticks to the knife return to the oven without the foil for 5 minutes.

Allow to stand for a few minutes, unmould and serve. You can decorate your dish with fresh parsley or a bunch of cress if you wish.

Courgettes Farcies à la Grecque
Greek Stuffed Courgettes

This is a favourite Greek dish and is called Papoutsakia, *or shoes. When I was in Bonn, my chef Nicholas Lagos, who was the King of Greece's chef until the Colonels' coup, gave me his recipe. We now serve it in Paris, with great success. Lagos, incidentally, locked up all the food which was in the royal kitchens when the Colonels' men stormed the Palace and refused to give up the keys. The soldiers eventually pushed the old gentleman aside (avoiding his carving knife) and plundered his stores. He was fired, never received a pension, and still trembles with anger when he tells the tale.*

SERVES 8

16 small courgettes
80 g (2½ oz) butter for béchamel
250 g (9 oz) flour
500 ml (scant pint) warm milk
100 g (3½ oz) fresh, warm cream
salt and pepper
yolks of 2 eggs
2 whole eggs
1 dessertspoon parsley, chopped
1 teaspoon basil, chopped
200 g (7 oz) grated cheese
200 g (7 oz) breadcrumbs
200 g (7 oz) grated Cheddar or
  Parmesan cheese
40 g (1½ oz) butter, melted

1 large pan for boiling
1 medium-sized heavy-bottomed
  pan for béchamel
1 baking dish

Top and tail the courgettes and cut them in half lengthwise. Criss-cross the centre of each half. Place the courgettes in a saucepan of boiling water and cook for 8–9 minutes. When they are cooked – they should be tender but not break – pour cold water over them to cool, and drain. Carefully spoon out the inside flesh of the courgettes and chop this up. Leave the shells upside down to drain.

Melt the butter to make a béchamel. Add the flour, cook it in the butter for about 3 minutes, then slowly pour in the milk. Allow to boil for 5 minutes over a gentle flame, stirring all the time. Remove from fire, add the cream, salt and pepper, the egg yolks and the whole eggs, the parsley and basil, and the flesh of the courgettes. Add grated cheese (we use a mixture of Cheddar or Parmesan with Stilton) and mix well.

Fill the courgette shells with this mixture. Place them in a greased baking dish, cover with the breadcrumbs mixed with more grated cheese and pour over the melted butter. Place in a preheated, very hot oven – 240 °C (450 °F)/Mark 9 – and bake until they are golden. (As an added finesse, Monsieur Lagos would pipe the courgette mixture into the shells. It makes the dish more decorative.)

Pâté de Faisan du Chef
The Chef's Pheasant Pâté

We serve this at large buffets and sometimes as a main course, accompanied by a Sauce Cumberland (page 122).

SERVES 6

1 pheasant
100 ml (7 dessertspoons) Madeira
50 ml (3½ dessertspoons) Cognac
jellied stock (page 173)
1 bowl for marinade

For the pâte à pâté:
300 g (11 oz) flour
80 g (scant 3 oz) butter
80 g (scant 3 oz) lard
2 heaped teaspoons salt
yolks of 2 eggs
200 ml (⅓ pint) water

300 g (10 oz) finely-minced pork
  (the chef prefers neck)
60 g (2 oz) pistachio nuts
salt, pepper and mixed spices
chopped parsley

1 sieve
1 bowl
1 pâté mould, 24 × 9 × 7 cm high
  (10 × 3½ × 3 in)

Skin the pheasant, keeping the liver, gizzard, etc. Cut the breast in strips and cut the meat off all the bones. Remove all gristle and marinate the pheasant meat in the Madeira and Cognac.

Prepare a jellied stock (page 173). (You can, of course, use canned bouillon or consommé with gelatine, but if you have time and patience, the chef's method is better.)

To make the *pâte à pâté*, or pastry dough, sieve the flour into a bowl, make a well in the centre and add the butter, lard, salt, egg yolks and water. Knead to obtain a firm dough. Allow it to stand for 1 hour before rolling out and using to line a pâté mould. The shape of the mould can be of your choice. The easiest to use are the pâté moulds with removable sides but a cake tin will do, too.

Keep the strips of pheasant breast aside and mince the rest of the meat through a fine mincing blade. Add this to the minced pork and mix in the pistachio nuts, the mixed spices and the marinade juices. Spread one layer of the mixture in the mould, then add one layer of the breast strips. Repeat until mould is filled, ending with a layer of the mince. Place in a moderate oven, 180 °C (350 °F)/Mark 4, for about 50 minutes. Allow to cool and then pour in the jellied stock. Cover and keep refrigerated until required.

Before serving, scatter a little chopped parsley over the pâté for decoration.

Tarte Barcelona
Barcelona Spinach Tart

We were served this tart in a restaurant in Barcelona and I find it makes an excellent first course – or, without the tart shell, spinach cooked this way makes a very original vegetable dish which we serve with roast beef.

SERVES 6–8

350 g (12 oz) shortcrust pastry

1 25-cm (10-in) tart tin

1.5 kg (3½ lb) fresh spinach
50 g (1¾ oz) butter for béchamel
60 g (2 oz) flour, sifted
250 ml (½ pint) hot milk
½ teaspoon nutmeg
25 g (¾ oz) butter
100 g (3½ oz) sultanas
60 g (2 oz) pine seeds
freshly-ground black pepper

1 large pan of boiling water
1 sieve
1 medium-sized saucepan for béchamel
1 small heavy pan

Prepare the shortcrust pastry (see master recipe, page 178). Cook tart shell (see method, page 33) and keep warm.

Thoroughly wash the spinach and cook it for about 5 minutes in plenty of lightly-salted boiling water in a covered pan. (The chef reckons 7 g (1 teaspoon) salt to 1 litre (2 pints) water.) Drain very thoroughly (this is essential) and chop. Cooking time for spinach depends on quality.

Make a béchamel with the butter, the flour and the milk, then add the nutmeg and spinach. Re-heat, allowing the spinach to boil for about 2 minutes. Heat the remaining butter in a small pan and toss the sultanas and pine seeds in this. Drain, then add the seeds and sultanas to the spinach and fill the warm tart shell with the mixture. Serve immediately.

You can add poached eggs on top of the tart, allowing one for each guest, if you wish. Sprinkle each egg with a pinch of freshly-ground black pepper.

Tarte aux Poireaux
Leek Tart

There are several ways of making this traditional dish. This is my own adaptation and I like it because it has a stronger leek flavour, which is brought out by the onions and the larger quantity of leeks used.

SERVES 8

2 kg (4½ lb) leeks
500 g (1 lb) white onions
100 g (3½ oz) fresh butter
1 litre (2 pints) stock (page 174)
salt and pepper
350 g (12 oz) shortcrust pastry
   (page 178)
200 ml (¾ pint) fresh cream
yolk of 6 eggs

1 heavy-bottomed pan with lid
1 25-cm (10-in) tart tin
greaseproof paper
dry white baking beans

Wash the leeks and peel the onions. Grate or chop them very, very finely. Put the onion and leek mixture in a heavy pan with the butter and one-quarter of the stock, cover with a lid and simmer until all the liquid has been absorbed. Add the rest of the stock and repeat until all the stock has been absorbed. Check the flavour, add salt and pepper to taste and allow to cool.

To prepare the tart, line a greased tin with the pastry and prick the base. Cover it with a piece of greaseproof paper and scatter over this some white baking beans. Bake in a preheated moderate oven, 200 °C (400 °F)/Mark 6, for about 15–20 minutes. The pastry should only just be cooked.

Add the cream and egg yolks to the onion and leek mixture and fill the tart. Bake for 15 minutes in a moderate oven, 200 °C (400 °F)/Mark 6. Allow the tart to stand for about 4 minutes before cutting into slices. If you wish you can add grated cheese on top, but that is not the traditional way to serve the dish.

Soufflé aux Œufs Pochés
Poached Egg Soufflé

SERVES 8

60 g (2 oz) butter
60 g (2 oz) flour, sifted
400 ml (⅔ pint) milk
salt
pinch nutmeg
180 g (6 oz) Cheddar cheese,
    grated
5 eggs, separated
8 poached eggs (page 172)

1 medium-size pan for béchamel
1 oval earthenware or porcelain
    dish, about 35 cm (14 in) long

This is an intriguing dish. Sir Christopher Soames (now Lord Soames) used to serve it and just to make it even more delicious he told the chef to scatter a few truffles round the eggs. After the Berrill report (which recommended that the Foreign Office should be abolished) we do not go in for such delicacies, and the chef mentions them with nostalgia!

Make a béchamel with the butter, flour, milk, salt and nutmeg (page 121). Remove from the heat and add 120 g (4 oz) cheese and the egg yolks one by one. Allow to cool and fold in the beaten whites. Half fill the buttered dish with this mixture, then place the poached eggs on top and cover with the remainder of the mixture. Scatter the remaining grated cheese over the top and place in a preheated very hot oven, 240 °C (475°F)/Mark 9 for 15 minutes. Serve immediately.

The chef has a very neat touch which helps guests find their eggs. He puts some of the soufflé mixture into a forcing bag and designs a rosette over each egg before scattering the cheese.

Mousse aux Quatre Fromages
Four Cheese Mousse

SERVES 5

50 g (1¾ oz) Stilton, pounded into a paste
50 g (1¾ oz) Cheddar, thinly grated
50 g (1¾ oz) Parmesan, thinly grated
50 g (1¾ oz) Gruyère, thinly grated
750 ml (1½ pints) fresh cream, beaten
yolks of 5 hard-boiled eggs, finely chopped
1 soupspoon fresh parsley, chopped
8 g (¼ oz) gelatine
100 ml (⅕ pint) hot water
1 soupspoon chives, finely chopped

1 mixing bowl
1 soufflé dish 15 cm (6 in) in diameter
greaseproof paper
string

Although hot soufflés are delicious, they are too delicate to serve for a large number of people. And the Embassy, although modernized in some respects since the days of Pauline Borghese, still has a kitchen which is too far from the dining rooms or salons which we turn into dining rooms for different occasions. With the modern housewife in mind, there is everything to be said for something that you can prepare in advance and that will not sink! Here is the chef's favourite cheese soufflé.

Mix the cheeses with the cream, add the egg yolks, the parsley and salt and pepper to taste. Dissolve the gelatine in the hot water, add and mix well.

Wrap a strip of double greaseproof paper around the outside of the soufflé dish. The paper should be long enough for the ends to overlap, and deep enough to extend from the bottom of the dish to about 5 cm (2 in) above the rim. Secure the paper collar with a piece of string. Pour in the mixture and leave in the refrigerator for 24 hours. To serve remove the collar carefully, decorate the top with a little parsley, chives and extra slices of hard-boiled egg.

In France, where the cream tends to be very thick, you can dilute it with a little milk. You need stiff cream but not too stiff, as you would not be able to mix all the ingredients.

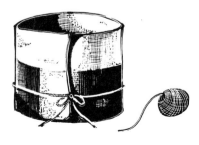

Œufs Écossais
Scotch Eggs

We like to serve these cut in half, to decorate our buffet dishes, or for a cold supper arranged in a nest of watercress. We serve a sauce tartar with them (page 128). They are a traditional English pub dish but quite an innovation in Paris in Pauline Borghese's gilt salons!

SERVES 8
8 eggs
6 heaped dessertspoons flour, sifted
1 teaspoon salt
500 g (1 lb) pork sausagemeat
1 egg, beaten
6 dessertspoons roasted breadcrumbs
vegetable oil for deep frying

1 saucepan
plates for flour, beaten egg and breadcrumbs
1 deep frying pan

Boil 8 eggs for 10 minutes, crack them and allow them to cool in cold water. Roll each cold hard-boiled egg in the flour sifted with the salt, then flatten out some sausagemeat, place the egg in the middle, fold the meat round the egg and press it into a ball. Coat all eggs in this way, then dip the egg balls first into the remaining flour, then into the beaten egg and finally into the breadcrumbs. Roll each egg well each time so that it is well coated. Fry the balls in deep hot oil, turning them and allowing them to fry slowly until they are a rich golden colour (about 4 minutes). Remove and drain. Cool and serve cold slit in half, decorated with parsley or watercress.

Soupe de Concombre Glacée
Iced Cucumber Soup

This is an ideal summer soup. It is easy to make and should be made in advance. The mint should be fresh – we grow ours in the Embassy garden.

SERVES 8

500 ml (scant pint) sour cream
140 ml (¼ pint) yoghourt
750 ml (1½ pints) pale ale
salt and pepper
2 cucumbers, diced
chopped fresh mint

1 earthenware bowl

Mix the sour cream, yoghourt and ale in a bowl, stirring until it is no longer frothy. Add salt and pepper to taste and the diced cucumbers. Allow to stand in a refrigerator for at least a day. Before serving, add chopped fresh mint; if the soup is too thick, dilute with a little cold milk. On special occasions you can, if you wish, sprinkle a little smoked cod's roe on top of each cup of soup.

Gazpacho

There are many variations of this Spanish soup. This is one we served in Madrid, where I had to remind my cook to be careful with the garlic – remembering Mrs Beeton's glorious understatement about it: 'Unless sparingly used the flavour is disagreeable to the palate'. In Paris the chef knows about the palate but you can, of course, omit the garlic and, if you wish, add a pinch of cumin. The chef likes to add cumin but it is all a question of taste. Gazpacho is an ideal summer soup and we serve it on hot nights when we dine in the romantic Embassy garden or in the glazed gallery looking out on to the garden. The gallery was added in 1826, when Lady Granville gave glittering Embassy parties. The architect was Luigi Visconti, who later designed Napoleon's tomb in the Invalides and the two new wings of the Louvre.

SERVES 6

4 ripe tomatoes
2 small cucumbers
3 green peppers (optional)
1 clove of garlic
6 dessertspoons olive oil
3 dessertspoons vinegar
4 slices bread
1 litre (2 pints) water
½ teaspoon paprika
1 dessertspoon salt

1 earthenware mixing bowl
1 liquidizer
1 sieve

To serve:
1 hard-boiled egg
1 firm tomato
½ cucumber
1 small onion

Cut the tomatoes into thick slices, slice the cucumbers, slice the peppers and remove the seeds, and crush the garlic. Put all these ingredients into a large bowl and pour into it the oil and vinegar, the bread, water, paprika and salt. Leave it to stand for about an hour or so, then blend all the ingredients in the liquidizer. If you wish to have a very smooth soup – and I like it that way – strain it through a fine sieve. Chill the soup in the refrigerator and serve very cold. You can, if you wish, put an ice cube into each soup plate and pour the gazpacho over it. Accompany the soup with the finely diced cucumbers, tomatoes, hard-boiled egg and finely chopped onion served on individual small plates.

At Baron Philippe de Rothschild's table, gazpacho is served with a sauceboat of a curry mayonnaise (curry powder added to the mayonnaise) and each guest takes a spoon of this and mixes it with his gazpacho. It gives the soup a delicious piquant flavour and is an original touch.

Bortsch Russe
Russian Bortsch

There are several ways to make this Russian dish, but the chef's recipe is light and excellent. We serve it at Christmas parties and buffets. It differs, of course, from the Polish Barszcz which usually omits the beef stock.

SERVES 10

1 small duck
350 g (12 oz) uncooked beetroot
250 g (9 oz) leeks
100 g (3½ oz) fennel
100 g (3½ oz) parsley roots
200 g (7 oz) white cabbage
800 g (1¾ lb) breast of beef
2.5 litres (5 pints) water
5 peppercorns
salt
sprig parsley
1 bayleaf
400 ml (⅔ pint) beetroot juice (see method)
250 ml (½ pint) sour cream

1 roasting tin
1 large saucepan
1 soup tureen

Half roast the duck in a preheated moderate oven – 200 °C (400 °F)/Mark 6 – and remove the fat. Thinly slice all the vegetables *en julienne* and stew gently in the duck fat in a covered pan for about 5 minutes. Add the beef and the duck, the water, the crushed peppercorns, salt, and, in a muslin bag, the parsley and the bayleaf. Cook very gently for 2½–3 hours, removing the herbs halfway through the cooking time. Cool and remove the fat from the bouillon.

Make the beetroot juice by grating and pressing another 600 g (1 lb 4 oz) raw beetroot. Dice the beef and duck. Place these in the bottom of the soup tureen, and add half the beetroot juice, the bouillon and half the vegetables. Serve, separately, one sauceboat with the remaining beetroot juice, and another with sour cream.

You can, if you wish, add 5 grilled chipolatas or small sausages with their skins removed and sliced. You can serve Pirojkis with the Bortsch.

Pirojkis

MAKES 18

1 onion, chopped
100 g (3½ oz) minced beef
50 g (1¾ oz) lean bacon
salt and pepper
1 teaspoon mixed herbs
350 g (12 oz) puff pastry (page 175)

1 small heavy-bottomed pan
1 oven tin
greaseproof paper

Lightly fry the onion until it is golden. Add the meat, bacon, salt and pepper, stir and cook for 3 minutes. Add the herbs.

Roll out the pastry and cut into circles 8 cm (3 in) in diameter. Spoon a little of the stuffing on to the centre of each circle and fold in half. Pinch the edges together and place in an oven tin lined with greaseproof paper. Cook in a preheated hot oven, 220 °C (425 °F)/Mark 7, for about 10 minutes. Serve hot with Bortsch.

Barszcz Polonais
Polish Barszcz

Polish Barszcz is a mixture of stock and sour beet juice thickened with soured cream. Here is my Polish cook's recipe which I use. It is the traditional peasant recipe. The sour beet juice must be prepared well in advance. It can be kept in the refrigerator and used when needed.

SERVES 8

6 medium-sized raw beetroots
2½ dessertspoons sugar
crusts of two slices brown bread

1 earthenware or glass jar with tight lid or cover

For the barszcz:
250 g (½ lb) soup bones
250 g (½ lb) mixed vegetables:
    60 g (2 oz) carrots
    20 g (⅔ oz) onions
    80 g (2¾ oz) leeks
    60 g (2 oz) celery
    30 g (1 oz) parsnips
4 medium-sized raw beetroots
salt and pepper
bayleaf
sprig of rosemary or juniper
sprig of parsley
2 cloves garlic
1 teaspoon mixed spices
2 teaspoons corn starch or sifted flour
250 ml (½ pint) soured cream
3 hard-boiled eggs, chopped (optional)

1 large pan with 3 litres (6 pints) water

Clean, skin and cut 6 beetroots into cubes. Place these in a jar and cover with warm water; the water should be boiled but tepid. Add the sugar and bread crusts. Cover the jar and leave in a warm place to ferment for 5–8 days. When the juice has fermented, pour it off and keep it in a cold place. Pour more warm water over the beetroots and leave this to ferment as before. Mix this with the juice from the first fermentation, pour into a jar and keep sealed in a cold place until you wish to use it. For the *barszcz* you will need 250 ml (½ pint) sour beet juice.

Clean the soup bones and vegetables, and wash, skin and quarter the remaining 4 beetroots (which should weigh about 300 g (10 oz)). Add salt, pepper, herbs, garlic and spices and simmer in the water for 1 hour. Strain. Mix the corn starch or flour with a little of the soured cream and stir into the stock to thicken, add 250 ml (½ pint) sour beet juice and bring to the boil. Adjust taste with a little sugar if you wish, or lemon juice. Serve hot or iced with a teaspoon of soured cream in each cup. I add a pinch of nutmeg too. For *Barszcz Tajkiem* you can add the chopped hard-boiled eggs before serving.

Note: If the *barszcz* is not red enough, grate another raw beetroot, place it in a colander and press the juice into the soup. My Polish cook used to hold the colander over the soup and press the beetroot with a spoon. Overcooking the *barszcz* results in the soup losing its red colour.

Consommé Grecque Avgolemono
Greek Avgolemono Consommé

It is always quite a problem to get guests to sit down for a large buffet dinner, and difficult, sometimes, to wait for latecomers. This often happens when we give parties for visiting ballet or theatre stars who have to change and take off their make-up — and yet they are the guests of honour.

One way we found was to offer a cup of consommé first. The waiters go round with a tray and guests help themselves. We did this for the Nureyev Gala in Paris and I was delighted to see that when he arrived he asked for his cup to be brim full and took a second helping. As the chef and I are always looking for something original, we serve the Avgolemono consommé on such occasions. Incidentally, it is of course an excellent and light first course for a small dinner.

SERVES 8
yolks of 8 eggs
juice of 2 lemons
1.5 litres (2¾ pints) chicken stock
little nutmeg (optional)

1 warm, preferably earthenware,
   mixing bowl or soup bowl
1 whisk

Beat the egg yolks and the lemon juice in the bowl with a whisk. Bring the chicken stock (sometimes we mix this with beef stock) to the boil and gradually pour over the yolk and lemon mixture, beating as you pour. Serve immediately in warmed soup cups, scattering a little nutmeg in each cup if you wish.

On a hot day this soup can be served chilled. When served hot as a first course the addition of a little rice and the diced breast of chicken makes it even more delicious. The rice and the chicken can be lightly cooked in the stock.

Potage Saint Germain
Saint Germain Soup

This is a favourite summer soup which we serve for buffets and dinners. It is easy to make and can be made well in advance. It is delicious hot, too.

SERVES 8
600 g (1¼ lb) fresh young garden
   peas
1.25 litres (2½ pints) milk
2 sprigs mint
salt to taste

1 medium-sized saucepan
1 strainer
1 mixing bowl
1 liquidizer
1 fine sieve

Cook the peas with 1 sprig of mint in the pan in about 4 litres (7 pints) salted water. Boil for 10 minutes or less, depending on quality of peas. They must remain a clear green colour. Strain and add 250 ml (½ pint) milk. Put the soup through the liquidizer and then through a very fine sieve or strainer. Add the remainder of the milk. Cut the leaves of the second sprig of mint into thin strips, add these to the soup and leave in refrigerator for 4 hours at least. Serve very cold.

LE DEPART.

Guéri du spleen par la Cuisine Française, l'Anglais retourne à Londres en embonpoint

.... Cured of 'the spleen' by French cuisine, a somewhat stouter Englishman returns to London

LES POISSONS

FISH DISHES

The Chef's Purses	Les Bourses du Chef
Salmon Coulibiac (Koulibiac)	Coulibiac de Saumon
Small Crab Soufflés	Petits Soufflés au Crabe
Smoked Salmon Pancakes	Crêpes Farcies au Saumon Fumé
Smoked Haddock Pancakes	Crêpes au Haddock Fumé
Haddock Mousse	Mousse de Haddock
Fresh Salmon Mousse	Mousse de Saumon Frais
Haddock Soufflé	Soufflé au Haddock
Bass Flambé with Fennel	Loup Flambé au Fenouil
Angler Pie	Croûte de Lotte
Puff Pastry Shell	Croûte Feuilletée
Red Mullet in Papillotes	Rouget en Papillotes
Red Mullet Pâté with Nantua Sauce	Pâté de Rouget Sauce Nantua
Haddock or Salmon Kedgeree	Kedgeree de Haddock ou de Saumon
Taramosalata	Taramosalata
Seafood Noodles	Nouilles aux Fruits de Mer
Indian Angler Fish with Almonds	Lotte aux Amandes à l'Indienne

Les Bourses du Chef
The Chef's Purses

This is my invention, and an adaptation of Eggs in Purses (page 25). We serve it to amuse bankers and businessmen, as it is an unusual dish which helps move the conversation off finance. It is a real example of Anglo-French cuisine, the smoked haddock being very English, the delicate presentation very French. The sauce inside the purses prevents the haddock and hard-boiled egg becoming too dry. We also serve a sauce separately.

SERVES 6

500 g (1 lb) smoked haddock
500 ml (scant pint) milk
30 g (1 oz) butter
30 g (1 oz) flour
freshly-ground pepper
3 hard-boiled eggs, chopped in
    large pieces
250 g (9 oz) *fondue de tomate
    Portugaise* (page 126)
12 small pancakes, about 15 cm
    (6 in) in diameter (page 179)
vegetable oil for deep frying
chopped parsley, lemon slices to
    decorate

1 pan with lid to poach haddock
1 heavy-bottomed pan for
    béchamel
1 mixing bowl
1 pan for deep frying
string

Pour boiling water over the smoked haddock and leave for 2–3 minutes. Drain and poach the fish in the milk in a covered pan for 10 minutes on a low heat. When the haddock is cooked, drain and flake. Keep milk for béchamel. (Cooking time for haddock depends on thickness and quality. In France the fish is often very thick and needs more cooking. The chef brings the haddock and milk to the boil and removes the pan to the side of the stove to simmer very gently.)

Make a kind of béchamel (page 121) with the butter and flour and the milk the haddock has been cooked in. Do not use salt, as the milk is already salty. If it is too salty, pour some of it off and fill up with fresh milk. Add freshly-ground pepper.

Mix the haddock with the eggs, the *fondue de tomate Portugaise* and 250 ml (½ pint) of the béchamel sauce. Place a spoonful of this mixture on the centre of each pancake and tie them with string in the shape of purses.

Plunge the purses in the hot oil and deep fry for about 2 minutes. Drain and cut the string. Serve on a warm serving dish which you can decorate with a carpet of chopped parsley and lemon slices. Serve the remainder of the sauce separately in a sauce boat.

Coulibiac de Saumon
Salmon Coulibiac

The chef uses 500 g (1 lb 2 oz) brioche dough for this. He omits the sugar and adds salt. You can, of course, use puff pastry but if you want to cut the cooked dish neatly before serving, the brioche pastry is easier to cut, the slices are neater and the brioche taste adds a rather special flavour to this classic Russian dish.

SERVES 8

100 g (3½ oz) semolina or
   long-grained rice
350 g (12 oz) salmon, sliced
100 g (3½ oz) butter
400 g (14 oz) mushrooms
250 g (9 oz) cooked, chopped
   sturgeon notochord, or tapioca
1 hard-boiled egg

For the pastry:
brioche dough made with 250 g
   (9 oz) flour (page 178)
3 dessertspoons melted butter
100 g (3½ oz) fresh breadcrumbs
2 dessertspoons chopped parsley

To serve:
200 g (7 oz) butter, melted
1 lemon

1 heavy pan for poaching salmon
1 large baking dish
1 pastry brush

Note: The notochord is the spinal cord of the sturgeon. It is an expensive ingredient and not absolutely necessary. The chef uses it when he is making coulibiac for dinner parties. It should be soaked for 5 hours, then cooked in slightly salty water for another 3 hours, then chopped. For less formal occasions, the chef uses large-grained tapioca called Japanese pearls, cooked in a little bouillon or salted water.

All the ingredients for the coulibiac should be cooked and cold; all the ingredients for the brioche should be warm – not hot or cold.

Boil the rice, drain and allow to cool. Toss the salmon in the hot butter for 3 minutes, then season to taste. Slice the mushrooms, lightly fry them in oil, and drain. Prepare the sturgeon or tapioca according to instructions above. Hard boil and chop the egg.

Roll out the dough into a rectangle about 30 × 18 cm (12 × 7 in). Starting with the cooked rice, spread all the ingredients for the filling in layers lengthwise along the centre of the dough.

Finally, draw up all the ends of the dough, folding them inwards, wet and seal together. Place the coulibiac on a baking dish with the join downwards, make a hole in the top to let the steam escape and leave for twenty minutes so the pastry dough can settle. Then, using a pastry brush, cover with melted butter, and sprinkle with fresh breadcrumbs and chopped parsley. Bake at 200 °C (400 °F)/Mark 6 for 45 minutes.

Serve with melted butter to which the juice of 1 lemon has been added, and chopped parsley.

Petits Soufflés au Crabe
Small Crab Soufflés

This is a light and original French way of serving crab.

SERVES 8

50 g (1¾ oz) butter
1 small onion, finely chopped
250 g (½ lb) crab meat
2 tomatoes, skinned, seeded and
  chopped
1 dessertspoon curry powder
450 ml (¾ pint) milk
150 g (5 oz) flour
60 g (2 oz) grated cheese
yolks of 5 eggs
salt and pepper
whites of 6 eggs, stiffly beaten
600 ml (1 pint) fresh cream
chopped parsley to garnish

1 small heavy pan with lid
1 large heavy-bottomed pan
16 small moulds, 7 cm (3 in)
  long, 5 cm (2 in) wide and 3 cm
  (1¼ in) high
1 35-cm (14-in) oval dish

Put 20 g (1 dessertspoons) butter in a small pan, add the onion, then the crab, tomato and curry powder. Cover and heat to boiling point, then remove from the fire and allow to sweat for about 5 minutes. Boil the milk in a large pan and add the flour, stirring vigorously with a wooden spatula. Add the remaining butter and the cheese, the egg yolks, the crab mixture, and salt and pepper to taste. Cool and fold in the stiffly-beaten egg whites. Fill individual greased moulds with this mixture and place them in a baking dish. Add a little water to the baking dish and place in a moderate oven, 200 °C (400 °F)/Mark 6 for 15 minutes.

Unmould the soufflés and place them in a well-buttered oval serving dish, cover with fresh cream and return to a preheated very slow oven (we leave our door open) for 15 minutes. The soufflés are ready when they have absorbed the cream. Serve immediately and scatter a little chopped parsley over them if you wish.

Crêpes Farcies au Saumon Fumé
Smoked Salmon Pancakes

At the Russian Embassy in Bonn I had thin strips of smoked salmon served separately with very light blini and this gave me the idea for these pancakes.

SERVES 6
500 ml (scant pint) pancake batter
  (page 179)
200 g (7 oz) fresh or sour cream
500 g (1 lb) smoked salmon
50 g (1¾ oz) melted butter
Hollandaise sauce with 6 egg
  yolks (page 123)
2 lemons
1 bunch watercress

1 heavy pancake pan
1 mixing bowl
1 oven dish
foil paper

Make 12 pancakes, using very little salt in the batter. Either buy soured cream or make your own by adding the juice of a quarter of a lemon to the fresh cream and allowing it to stand in the warm kitchen for about 2 hours.

Cut the salmon into narrow strips about 5 cm (2 in) long. Mix them in the melted butter, place on the pancakes and roll. Arrange the pancakes in a buttered dish, cover with foil and heat in a moderately hot oven, 200 °C (400 °F)/Mark 6, for 5 minutes.

Pour over the Hollandaise sauce and put the dish under the grill or in a hot oven for a few minutes to brown. Serve immediately, decorated with lemon slices and a bunch of watercress. Pass round the sour cream separately.

Crêpes au Haddock Fumé
Smoked Haddock Pancakes

These are cheaper than the smoked salmon pancakes and are very, very good.

SERVES 6

500 ml (scant pint) pancake batter (page 179)
500 g (1 lb) smoked haddock
500 ml (scant pint) milk
1 dessertspoon *fondue de tomate Portugaise* (page 126)
25 g (1 oz) butter
35 g (1½ oz) flour

1 heavy pancake pan
1 medium-sized pan to cook haddock
1 oven dish
1 small pan for béchamel

Make 12 pancakes, using very little salt in the batter. Set aside.

Pour boiling water over the smoked haddock and leave for 2–3 minutes. Remove, drain and poach in the milk in a covered pan for 10 minutes (page 44). Drain, reserving the milk, and flake. Mix the fish with the *fondue de tomate Portugaise*.

Fill the pancakes with the smoked haddock mixture and place them in a buttered dish. Cover with foil and bake in a preheated moderately hot oven, 200 °C (400 °F)/Mark 6, for 10 minutes.

While the pancakes are in the oven, make a béchamel sauce (page 121) using the butter, flour and reserved milk. (The béchamel takes the place of the Hollandaise in the preceding recipe; if you want a more refined sauce, add the yolk of 1 egg so as to make it into a kind of Hollandaise.) Remove the dish from the oven, pour over the sauce and serve immediately.

Mousse de Haddock
Haddock Mousse

This is an easy dish to prepare in advance for a buffet or an entrée.

SERVES 6–8

500 ml (scant pint) jellied fish
  stock (page 174)
12 black olives, halved
4 hard-boiled eggs
300 g (10 oz) haddock
500 ml (1 pint) milk
250 ml (½ pint) béchamel (page
  121)
250 ml (½ pint) mayonnaise (page
  124)
250 ml (½ pint) fresh cream
salt and pepper
1 bunch watercress

1 pastry brush
1 22.5-cm (9-in) ring mould
1 pan to cook haddock

Warm up a little jellied stock. Using a pastry brush, coat the
mould with the jellied stock and decorate the base with black
olives centred on the slices of 2 hard-boiled eggs. Poach the
haddock in the milk, allow to cool and flake. Add the fish to
the béchamel (make this with the milk in which you poached
the fish). Add the mayonnaise, the remaining 2 hard-boiled
eggs, chopped, and most of the cold jellied stock. (The latter
must not be too hard – the chef describes the consistency as
rather similar to the unbeaten whites of eggs.) Beat the cream –
not too stiffly – and fold in. Add salt and pepper to taste. Pour
into the prepared mould and place in the refrigerator for 4
hours.

To unmould, dip in hot water and turn out. Decorate with a
bunch of watercress in the centre and the remaining jellied
stock, cut into little lozenges.

Mousse de Saumon Frais
Fresh Salmon Mousse

We serve this dish with the Scotch salmon we have flown into Paris, and call it Mousse de Saumon d'Écosse. *In the Embassy it is prepared in a fish mould and guests have referred to it as being far too beautiful to eat.*

The mould is lightly coated with jelly made from fish stock. The mousse is then poured into the mould and left in the refrigerator for at least 4 hours. To unmould the mousse, the chef dips the mould rapidly in hot water and turns it out on a dish already prepared with a bed of jelly. He then goes to work on the decoration. Very thin slices of unpeeled cucumber cut into four are arranged like scales – starting from the tail and working towards the head. A round slice of hard-boiled egg yolk and a round cut out of half a black olive form the eye. The fins, the mouth and the tail are decorated with butter, using an icing nozzle, and sometimes the chef mixes a little tomato ketchup with the butter for colour. The serving dish is decorated with a ring of thin lemon slices and, on special occasions, the chef dots the dish with quail's eggs lightly sprinkled with paprika or chopped parsley, laid in tiny 'nests' of cucumber slices. A sauce verte *(page 128) is served with this dish.*

If you have time to make the jellied fish stock for this dish after you have cooked the salmon, use the court bouillon, *strained, instead of water. However, it is far more practical to make jellied stock in advance, and keep it until needed.*

SERVES 8
For the court bouillon:
1 carrot, sliced
1 onion, quartered
1 *bouquet garni* (thyme, parsley, bay leaf)
2 peppercorns
500 g (1 lb) salmon
250 ml (scant ½ pint) béchamel
5 dessertspoons jellied fish stock (page 174)
salt and pepper
150 ml (¼ pint) fresh cream
slices of unpeeled cucumber

Make a *court bouillon* from 1 litre (2 pints) water, the carrot, onion, *bouquet garni* and peppercorns.

Simmer for 1 hour and allow to cool. Strain before using, then gently simmer the fresh salmon in the liquid for 15 minutes. (You can, if you wish, use cooked salmon and avoid this stage.) Drain and flake the salmon, reserving the *court bouillon* for the fish stock, if you wish to make it up fresh.

Put the flaked salmon and béchamel into a liquidizer and then through a fine sieve. Add 5 dessertspoons cold jellied fish stock, a pinch of salt and pepper, and fold in the lightly beaten cream. Pour into a prepared soufflé dish (page 35) and place in the refrigerator for at least 4 hours. Remove the paper from the soufflé case and decorate the top with cucumber slices,

1 saucepan
1 fish kettle
1 liquidizer
1 fine sieve
1 soufflé dish, 18 cm (7 in) in
    diameter and 9 cm (3½ in) high
greaseproof paper
string

chopped aspic or sliced hard-boiled egg.

If a fish mould is used, this must be lightly coated with slightly warmed jellied fish stock using a pastry brush, and decoration follows the unmoulding.

A mousse made from smoked salmon is equally good. Prepare it in the same way, using 250 g (9 oz) smoked salmon, 300 ml (½ pint) béchamel, 500 ml (scant pint) jellied fish stock, and 150 ml (¼ pint) fresh cream.

Soufflé au Haddock
Haddock Soufflé

This is a light first course for lunch. We serve it at small lunches, sometimes accompanied by a tomato sauce (page 126) to which we add tomato ketchup and sherry, or, more frequently, with some of the sauce used in the soufflé to which we add a pinch of paprika and a little curry powder.

SERVES 6
350 g (12 oz) smoked haddock
500 ml (scant pint) milk
80 g (2¾ oz) butter
60 g (2 oz) flour
pepper
2 tomatoes
1 small onion, chopped
1 small clove garlic, crushed
yolks of 3 eggs
whites of 4 eggs, stiffly beaten

1 pan to poach haddock
1 heavy pan for sauce
1 small pan for tomatoes
1 mixing bowl
1 soufflé dish 18 cm (7 in) in
    diameter

Poach the haddock in simmering milk for about 10 minutes. When cold, drain and flake. Keep the milk for the sauce.

For the white sauce, make a *roux*, as the French say – that is, cook 50 g (1¾ oz) butter and the flour until it is a golden brown colour and then add the liquid, in this case the milk the haddock has cooked in. Stir until smooth, add pepper (the haddock will have supplied sufficient salt) and simmer gently for 10 minutes.

Skin the tomatoes by dropping them in boiling water for a few seconds, then seed and chop them. Place them in a small pan and cook gently with the remaining butter, the onion and garlic. Remove from the fire and add 200 ml (⅓ pint) of the white sauce and the flaked haddock. Mix and turn out into a bowl and, when cool, add the egg yolks one at a time. Finally fold in the well-beaten whites. Pour into a prepared soufflé dish (page 35) and cook in a moderately hot oven, 200 °C (400 °)/Mark 6, for about 20 minutes. Serve immediately.

If you have some of the sauce left over, either serve it separately in a sauce boat or use it over another egg dish. For instance, coat some *oeufs mollets* or pour the sauce over sliced hard-boiled eggs. Decorate with watercress and scatter a little paprika over the eggs. (For *oeufs mollets* see page 172.)

Loup Flambé au Fenouil
Bass Flambé with Fennel

This is quite a tour de force *— as it comes into the dining room in flames, smelling deliciously of fennel. When we have dinner parties at small tables and there are five or six of these large fish, there is no trouble with the conversation.*

SERVES 8

1 bass, weighing about 1.5 kg (3½ lb)
salt and pepper
6 fresh fennel (Florence fennel or finocchi)
200 g (7 oz) fillet of sole
2 teaspoons powdered fennel
400 g (14 oz) butter
150 ml (¼ pint) olive oil
200 g (7 oz) fried breadcrumbs (see method)
200 ml (⅓ pint) vegetable oil
150 g (5 oz) dried fennel branches
300 ml (½ pint) brandy

1 medium-sized pan
1 mortar or liquidizer
1 sieve
1 70 × 50 cm (28 × 20 in) sheet of greaseproof paper

Scale, clean and bone the bass, then wash and dry it. (Split it open down the back to bone.) Add salt and pepper.

Peel the fennel, wash and poach them in lightly boiling salted water for 15 minutes. Put the fennel and the sole fillets through a sieve (either pound them before or put them in the liquidizer), add salt and pepper to taste, half the powdered fennel and 100 g (3½ oz) butter, melted. Stuff the bass with this mixture.

Prepare the greaseproof paper by covering it with the olive oil, and scatter a little salt and pepper and powdered fennel over it. Wrap the bass in this, folding back the paper to leave the head and tail outside. Oil the outside of the paper with a pastry brush and place the bass in a moderate oven, 200 °C (400 °F)/Mark 6, for 45 minutes.

Fry the breadcrumbs in 50 g (3 dessertspoons) butter and the vegetable oil, drain and put through a fine sieve.

When the bass is cooked cut off the top part of the paper, leaving the fish resting on the paper underneath it. Remove the skin and the brown flesh (this is the fat of the bass). Spread the fried breadcrumbs over the white flesh, place the bass on a hot serving dish and arrange the branches of fennel all around it. Heat up the brandy and just before serving pour it over the bass and the fennel and set alight. Serve with the remaining butter, melted, in a sauce boat, to which you have added powdered fennel and chopped parsley. You can decorate your serving dish with slices of lemon if you wish.

Croûte de Lotte
Angler Pie

This makes a good informal dinner dish. We served it to the late, aged and gifted painter, Duncan Grant, when he came to Paris in a wheelchair to visit the Cézanne exhibition. He found this angler pie light, tasty and very French.

SERVES 6

1.5 kg (3½ lb) angler
45 g (3 dessertspoons) flour
2 dessertspoons oil
40 g (1½ oz) butter
30 g (1 oz) shallots, chopped
100 ml (7 dessertspoons) brandy
500 ml (scant pint) white wine
400 g (14 oz) fresh tomatoes, or
    40 g (2½ dessertspoons)
    concentrated tomato purée
1 dessertspoon chopped tarragon

For the liaison:
50 g (1¾ oz) butter
50 g (1¾ oz) flour

1 warm puff pastry shell using
    about 500 g (1 lb 2 oz) puff
    pastry (see page 54)

Cut the angler into pieces weighing about 40 g (1½ oz) each. Dip them into the flour and drop into a pan containing the hot oil and the butter. Cook to a golden colour. Add the shallots, and the Cognac set alight. Add the wine and the tomatoes and cook gently for 25 minutes. Drain the pieces of angler and keep them warm in a double boiler (*bain-marie*) while you boil up the sauce with the tarragon.

Thicken the sauce with what the French call a liaison (a mixture of flour and butter); in this case heat 50 g (1¾ oz) butter and add 50 g (1¾ oz) flour, stir and slowly add the angler sauce. Place the pieces of angler in the pastry shell, pour over half the sauce and serve the rest (strained) separately in a sauce boat. This dish is delicious with angler (or angle fish as it is called in America), but can of course be made with any firm white fish.

Croûte Feuilletée
Puff Pastry Shell

500 g (1 lb 2 oz) puff pastry (page 175)
yolk of 1 egg
1 dessertspoon milk

1 sharp knife
1 greased baking tin
1 pastry brush
greaseproof paper or foil

Divide 500 g (1 lb 2 oz) puff pastry dough into 2 portions. Roll out one piece to a thickness of about 4 mm ($\frac{1}{5}$ in) and cut a circle 22.5 cm (9 in) in diameter. Prick with a fork and wet the edges with a little cold water. Roll out the other half to a thickness of about 1.5 cm ($\frac{3}{4}$ in) and cut this in a circle of the same dimensions as the one above, then cut out of the centre a small circle measuring 15 cm (6 in) in diameter and discard.

You now have two pieces of puff pastry, one base and one crown. Place the crown over the base, mark with a knife to decorate and paint with a glaze made from the egg yolk mixed with the milk. Allow the pastry shell to rest before putting it in a preheated hot oven, 220 °C (425 °F)/Mark 7 for 20–25 minutes. If the shell is cooking too rapidly, cover with foil or paper.

Rouget en Papillotes
Red Mullet in Papillotes

This is an easy dish which looks grand and amusing. You can use it as a main course for a light dinner, beginning with a potage and ending with a sorbet. We serve it to our jet-propelled ministers when they arrive late for a light supper.

SERVES 6

6 red mullets weighing about
   300 g (10 oz) (or 12 weighing
   150 g (5 oz))
300 g (10 oz mushrooms, peeled
   and sliced
salt and pepper
2 teaspoons powdered fennel
2 dessertspoons chopped parsley
250 g (9 oz) butter
2 lemons

greaseproof paper cut into
   40 × 30 cm (16 × 12 in) strips
1 large ovenproof dish

Ask your fishmonger to clean, scale and bone the red mullet. If you are doing it yourself, scrape the fish with a sharp knife to remove scales, then open up the mullet along the back, starting from the tail and cutting close to the backbone.

Stuff the centres of the mullets with the mushrooms (lightly fried in butter and allowed to cool), add salt and pepper, a little fennel powder and some chopped parsley. Wrap each fish in an oiled strip of greaseproof paper, place in a greased oven dish and cook in a hot oven, 240°C (475°F)/Mark 9 for 10–15 minutes, depending on the size of the mullet.

Before serving open up the paper, scatter a little chopped parsley over the mullet and slip in a knob of butter (about 50 g (2 oz) altogether). Serve on a dish decorated with 1 lemon, sliced, and a big bunch of parsley.

Accompany with a sauce of 200 g (7 oz) clarified butter (page 153) to which you have added some chopped parsley, the juice of the remaining lemon, a little powdered fennel, and salt and pepper.

If you wish to simplify this dish, leave out the mushrooms and add more chopped parsley mixed with a few capers. You can then add a few capers to your sauce.

Pâté de Rouget Sauce Nantua
Red Mullet Pâté with Nantua Sauce

We very often serve a pâté as a first course, as it's a choice I often make when eating in a good restaurant. The chef's red mullet pâté is light and original.

SERVES 8

400 g (14 oz) red mullet fillets
2 teaspoons olive oil
salt and pepper
fennel powder

For the panade:
100 ml (3½ oz) milk
20 g (¾ oz) butter
50 g (1¾ oz) flour

For the stuffing:
300 g (10 oz) fillet of sole
salt and pepper
fennel powder
pinch saffron
1 dessertspoon chopped parsley

500 g (1 lb 2 oz) pie pastry (page 178)

1 small pan
1 liquidizer or mortar
1 fine sieve
1 mixing bowl
1 25-cm (10-in) pâté mould

Marinate the red mullet fillets in the oil with salt and pepper and a pinch of fennel powder.

Make a *panade*, or thick white sauce, by heating the milk and butter in a small pan. When boiling, remove from stove and add the flour. Mix rapidly, return to fire and stir to dry out mixture. Remove and allow it to cool.

To make the stuffing, add the *panade* to the sole fillets and pound or put into a liquidizer, then press through a fine sieve into a mixing bowl. Add salt and pepper, fennel powder, the saffron, and chopped parsley.

Line the pâté mould with pastry. Spread one layer of the stuffing on the bottom, then one layer of the red mullet fillets. Repeat in alternate layers, ending with a layer of stuffing. Cook for 35–40 minutes in a slow oven, 150 °C (330 °F)/Mark 2. Take the pâté out when cooked and allow it to stand for 10 minutes or so before cutting the slices. Serve hot on a bed of rice with small boiled potatoes with Nantua sauce (page 126).

The pâté is also delicious cold with a green sauce (page 128).

Kedgeree de Haddock ou de Saumon
Haddock or Salmon Kedgeree

Sir Christopher Soames, now Lord Soames, used to serve this dish at large supper parties and his French guests were always enthusiastic. What makes the traditional English dish rather special is the chef's idea to serve a sauce with it. Kedgeree can be dry – the chef's sauce makes amends.

SERVES 8

1.2 kg (2½ lb) fish (haddock or salmon, skinned)
1 litre (2 pints) milk
280 g (10 oz) rice
6 hard-boiled eggs, chopped and hot
100 g (3½ oz) butter, melted
pepper
½ lemon, sliced
chopped parsley

1 pan to poach haddock
1 pan for rice
1 earthenware bowl
1 ring mould or savarin mould, about 25 cm (10 in) in diameter

Poach the haddock or salmon in the milk over a gentle heat and in a covered pan (see page 44 for haddock). Drain, reserving the milk, flake the fish and keep warm.

Cook the rice in boiling salted water for 18 minutes, keeping it firm. Strain and place in an earthenware bowl. Add a quarter of the fish, 3 eggs chopped in large pieces, the melted butter, and pepper to taste. Press this mixture into a ring mould and upturn the mould on to the serving dish. Spoon the rest of the flaked fish pieces into the centre of the ring and add the remaining 3 hard-boiled eggs. Decorate the dish with rings of fresh lemon, cut if you wish with a crinkled cutter, and scatter over the chopped parsley.

Make a béchamel (page 121) with 500 ml (1 pint) of the milk you have used to poach the fish, and serve with the kedgeree.

You can, if you wish, serve the dish in the traditional way it was served by the British in India – that is, by spreading the rice and fish and eggs in alternate layers in a gratin dish, with a curry béchamel between the layers. For this you will need 750 ml (1½ pints) of béchamel with curry.

Taramosalata

This Greek dish can be made with smoked cod's roe or with grey mullet's roe. You can serve it in individual little pots decorated with black olives (halved and stoned) and accompanied by hot toast. Or you can serve a bowl of it at a small cocktail party and let guests dip into it themselves. We serve it sometimes as a sauce for a fish or egg dish and it is always a great success. There are many ways of making taramosalata. This method produces a very light dish.

SERVES 10

400 g (14 oz) smoked cod's roe
40 g (1½ oz) fresh white crustless
  bread, soaked in cold water
1 clove garlic (optional)
1 dessertspoon chopped shallots
  (optional)
300 ml (½ pint) vegetable oil
150 ml (¼ pint) olive oil
2 dessertspoons wine vinegar
juice of 2 lemons

1 bowl of warm water
1 mortar or cutter
1 mixer or whisk

Leave the cod's roe in a bowl of warm water for a few minutes. Then remove, drain, clean and skin. Squeeze out the cold water from the bread. Place the roe and the bread in a mortar (you can at this point add the garlic and shallots but we do not do this), and pound into a paste.

Place the cod's roe paste in a mixing bowl and gradually add the oil, vinegar and lemon juice as for a mayonnaise, beating all the time. You may wish to add 2 dessertspoons of water if the taramosalata is too thick. Beat well so that you obtain a very light, stiff pink cream.

Nouilles aux Fruits de Mer
Seafood Noodles

Home-made noodles do take time to make but they are very light and delicious. The chef's seafood dish is very fresh, very French and original. Palourdes, or carpet shells, are a great favourite with the French; if you cannot obtain these, use ordinary clams instead. Be sure all the shells are well scrubbed before cooking.

SERVES 8

250 ml (½ pint) dry white wine
1 small onion, chopped
1 clove garlic, chopped
1 *bouquet garni*
1.5 litres (3 pints) mussels

Heat the wine, onion, garlic and the *bouquet garni* in a pan, and put all the shells in this. Cover the pan and cook until the shells are open. Remove them and cook the prawns in the same liquid for 6 minutes, then remove and shell. Strain the cooking liquid through a piece of cheese cloth and pour into a mixing

500 ml (1 pint) cockles
16 *palourdes*
16 prawns
100 g (3½ oz) fresh cream
yolks of 4 eggs
juice of ½ lemon
800 g (1¾ lb) noodles, cooked
(page 106)
2 dessertspoons chopped parsley

1 large pan to cook seafood
cheesecloth
1 mixing bowl
1 medium bowl
1 medium-sized heavy pan for
sauce

bowl. Add the cream, egg yolks and the lemon juice and mix. Pour into a heavy pan, heat and bring to the boil but do not boil. Mix this sauce with the shelled seafood and noodles and the chopped parsley. You can serve immediately in a deep serving dish, or have a pastry case ready as on page 54 and serve the noodles in this. The chef does not add salt to the dish as the seafood are, he thinks, salty enough. Serve a bowl of grated Parmesan or Gruyère cheese separately to accompany the dish.

Lotte aux Amandes à l'Indienne
Indian Angler Fish with Almonds

SERVES 8

2 kg (4½ lb) angler fish
4 onions, chopped
150 g (5 oz) butter
salt and pepper to taste
1 teaspoon curcuma or ginger
pinch cinnamon
500 ml (scant pint) fresh cream
200 ml (⅓ pint) yoghourt
300 g (10 oz) blanched almonds,
pounded
lemon slices to garnish

1 heavy-bottomed pan

The chef likes this Indian dish as an entrée for a small dinner or a main course for a light lunch. In Paris we use angler fish, but any white firm fish can be used.

Cut the angler fish into pieces weighing about 90 g (3 oz) each. Gently fry the onions in the butter, keeping them golden and transparent, then add the angler, salt, pepper, cinnamon and curcuma. Pour in half the cream and cook until the cream has been absorbed, then add the rest of the cream, the yoghourt and the pounded almonds. Cook for a further 10 minutes and serve either in the centre of a ring of Indian rice, or in a pie shell as in the angler recipe on page 54. Decorate your dish with slices of lemon. For *Riz à l'Indienne* (Indian Rice) see page 107.

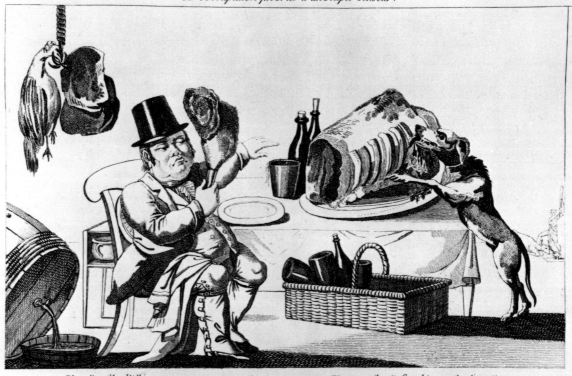

La Collation Anglaise,
ou l'occupation favorite d'un Peuple Penseur.

Plus d'un fils d'Albion au port grave et pesant,
Passe pour un penseur profond et pénétrant;
On se trompe en cela comme en toute autre affaire,
Milord ne pense pas, Messieurs, mais il digère

Et comme il sait fort bien que les distractions
Sont souvent un obstacle aux grandes fonctions,
D'un Estomac qu'il craint autant qu'il le révère,
Il ne veut pas troubler l'utile ministère.

A Paris, chez Martinet, Libraire, rue du Coq, No. 15.

The English snack, or the favourite occupation of a thinking people

LES VIANDES, POULETS, ET GIBIERS

MEAT, CHICKEN AND GAME

Lamb or Chicken Curry	Curry d'Agneau ou de Poulet
Baron of Lamb	Baron d'Agneau
Grandmother's Braised Leg of Mutton	Gigot Braisé Grand'mère
Leg of Lamb in Pastry	Gigot d'Agneau en Croûte
Baby Lamb with Sorrel	Agneau de Lait à l'Oseille
English Stuffed Shoulder of Lamb	Épaule d'Agneau Farcie à l'Anglaise
George V's Mutton Pie	Pie de Mouton George V
English Roast Beef with Yorkshire Pudding	Contre-filet à l'Anglaise avec Yorkshire Pudding
Fillet of Beef Wellington	Filet de Boeuf Wellington
Pickwick Pie	Pie Pickwick
Veal Belgrade	Veau Belgrade
Veal Cutlets St James	Cotelette de Veau St James
Veal Rolls with Olives	Rouleaux de Veau aux Olives
Victorian Veal Pie	Pie de Veau Victoria
Pork Pie	Pie au Porc
Sugar-Glazed Ham	Jambon Glacé au Caramel
York Ham with Parmesan Cheese	Jambon de York au Parmesan
Moussaka	Moussaka
Keftedes: Greek Meat Balls	Keftedes: Boules de Viande Grecques
Stuffed Cabbage Limousine	Chou Farci Limousine
Chicken and Macaroni Pie	Timbale de Macaroni au Poulet
Chilean Chicken Pie (Pastel de Choclo)	Poulet à la Chilienne
Duck with Peaches	Canard aux Pêches
Turkey Pie	Pie de Dinde
Game Pie	Pie de Gibier en Croûte
Pigeon Pie	Pie de Pigeon
Quail Pie	Pie de Cailles
Young Wild Boar Terrine	Terrine de Marcassin
Sauté Rabbit with Cider	Lapin Sauté au Cidre
Rabbit Back Dijonnais	Râble de Lapin Dijonnais

Curry d'Agneau ou Poulet
Lamb or Chicken Curry

We like to serve lamb curry for buffets and chicken curry for lunches. At buffets the various accompaniments are always appreciated and you can vary them as you wish. Curry is a dish which is easy to prepare for a large number of guests. In spite of the dazzling Empire décor in the British Embassy we serve the curry at buffets in the chef's copper pans. Curry must be hot and copper pans retain the heat and look very pretty.

SERVES 8–10

100 g (3½ oz) fresh butter

1.6 kg (3½ lb) lean shoulder of lamb or chicken, diced

200 g (7 oz) small onions, boiled for about 4 minutes

20 g (1 heaped dessertspoon) flour

30 g (2 dessertspoons) curry powder

4 apples, peeled, cored and diced

1 litre (2 pints) meat stock

salt

1 *bouquet garni*

40 g (2 heaped dessertspoons) coconut, freshly grated

100 g (3½ oz) fresh cream

2 dessertspoons chopped parsley to serve

1 large deep heavy casserole or stewing pan with lid

Heat the butter in the pan, toss the lamb or chicken pieces and the onion in the butter, scatter the flour over them and continue to *sauté* until the pieces are a golden colour. Then add the curry powder, apples, stock, salt and the *bouquet garni*. Cover and cook gently for 1 hour. Remove the *bouquet garni*, add the coconut and cook for a further 20 minutes (for chicken 10 minutes' further cooking is enough). Remove the meat or chicken pieces and keep warm. Spoon off the fat, add the cream to the cooking juices and bring the sauce to the boil. Check taste and add salt or curry powder if necessary.

Serve hot in a deep pan or dish, pouring the sauce over the meat or chicken pieces and scattering chopped parsley over the whole dish. Serve the remainder of the sauce separately.

This dish can be served with *Riz à l'Indienne* – Indian White Rice (page 107) – and an assortment of the following accompaniments: fried raisins, fried parsley, the chopped yolk and white of hard-boiled eggs, diced sweet peppers, freshly-grated coconut, thinly-sliced onions fried in butter, fried bananas, fried sliced almonds, fried cashew nuts, fried and thinly-sliced mushrooms, ginger marmalade, pickles and hot chutney sauce.

Baron d'Agneau
Baron of Lamb

This is a very popular dish in Paris, and I have seen it served in the most elegant houses. It is particularly good when served by the Rothschilds at Lafite or at Mouton, where the baby Pauillac lamb is even more tender and tasty as it feeds on the salty grass in the fields near the sea. Our chef serves the baron with elegance and has his special method of cooking it.

SERVES 8–10
1 baron of lamb
150 ml (¼ pint) vegetable oil
3 dessertspoons olive oil
50 g (2 dessertspoons) chopped onion
1 clove garlic, crushed and chopped
1 teaspoon crushed thyme
1 bayleaf, crushed
juice of 3 lemons
1 sheep's or pig's caul

1 large bowl for marinade
1 baking dish

For the sauce:
500 ml (scant pint) water
150 ml (¼ pint) dry white wine

1 small saucepan
1 fine strainer

Note: The lamb should be a baby lamb – milk fed and tender. A baron of lamb is the cut which includes the saddle and the two hind legs.

Twenty-four hours before you will be cooking the lamb, put the baron in a marinade made from the mixed oils and the onion, garlic, thyme, bayleaf and lemon juice.

Before cooking, envelop the baron in the caul. Then place it in a baking tin in the oven at 200 °C (400 °F)/Mark 6, basting very often with the marinating juices. For the correct cooking time you should reckon 20 minutes per 450 g (1 lb). (The chef uses a special, and in a way peasant, method of basting his meat. He makes up a little 'brush' with various twigs of herbs, dips this in the juices and then passes it over the joint. The meat is not only well basted in this way but also takes in the aroma of the herbs.)

When the baron is cooked, allow it to stand for 15 minutes, then cut the meat in thickish slices and put back on the carcass, in the correct order, so that the baron is served whole.

For the sauce, pour off the fat from the baking tin (a process known as *déglacer*), pour in 500 ml (scant pint) water and the dry white wine. Stir well to scoop up all the cooking juices. Heat, strain and serve in a sauce boat. The chef serves a second sauce with the baron – he likes the sauce Smitane (page 128). He decorates his dish with tomatoes *provençales* and asparagus tips (page 100), puts a frill on each leg bone and tucks a large bunch of watercress under the meat.

Gigot Braisé Grand'mère
Grandmother's Braised Leg of Mutton

This is a good winter dish. It is a traditional French farmhouse family dish which the chef serves with great elegance, and it tastes delicious. At the Embassy we import lamb and mutton from the UK – just to make the menu a little different and a little more British.

SERVES 9–10
200 g (7 oz) butter
1 leg of lamb or mutton,
    weighing 2 kg (4½ lb)
2 carrots, sliced
1 sprig celery
1 large onion, sliced
1 *bouquet garni*
2 dessertspoons concentrated
    tomato purée
3 litres (5 pints) meat stock
1 calf's foot, cut in 4 pieces
salt and pepper
1 dessertspoon cornflour
100 ml (⅓ pint) Madeira
200 g (7 oz) small white onions
200 g (7 oz) bacon

1 large heavy stewing pan or
    cocotte large enough to cook
    the leg
1 pan of cold water to scald calf's
    foot
1 strainer
1 small saucepan

Heat the butter in the stewing pan or cocotte, add the leg of mutton and turn it so that it browns all over. Remove the leg and, in the same butter, toss the carrots, celery, sliced onion and *bouquet garni*. Finally stir in the tomato purée. Place the leg of mutton in the stewing pan again and cover with the stock. Bring the calf's foot to the boil in a pan of cold water, remove and add it to the stewing pan together with salt and pepper to taste. Cook gently for 2 hours, covered, turning the leg over from time to time. When it is cooked, remove and keep warm.

Pour off the cooking juices and strain into a small saucepan. Mix the cornflour with the Madeira, pour into the juices, stir and cook for 3–4 minutes. Boil the small onions and cut the bacon in strips and blanch it for 4 minutes in boiling salted water. Add these to the sauce and allow it to simmer gently for 15 minutes, removing the fat as it comes to the surface. Strain off the bacon and onions and keep them warm.

Carve the leg and re-form, carefully placing the pieces back on the bone. Serve the leg on a warmed serving dish. Scatter the little onions and the bacon over it. Just before serving pour some of the sauce over the leg; serve the rest in a sauce boat.

The chef likes to serve round this dish groups of small potato and spinach soufflés (Potatoes Elizabeth, page 105) or Potato Nuts (page 104). He puts a frill on the bone and tucks a bunch of fresh watercress under it. He also serves a purée of brussels sprouts or a vegetable purée with this dish.

Gigot d'Agneau en Croûte
Leg of Lamb in Pastry

The French undercook lamb, the British tend to overcook it. The chef has compromised and serves it just slightly pink. The leg in pastry looks good and the pastry shell keeps all the goodness in. It is a pretty and amusing dish for a hot buffet.

SERVES 8–10

1 small leg of lamb, weighing about 2 kg (4½ lb)
1 clove garlic, crushed
2 dessertspoons oil
salt and freshly-ground black pepper
1 carrot, sliced
1 large onion, sliced
500 g (1 lb 2 oz) sausagemeat
200 g (7 oz) mushrooms, sliced and tossed in a little warm butter
1 medium-sized onion, chopped
1 dessertspoon parsley, finely chopped
1 teaspoon powdered rosemary (or 2 teaspoons fresh and finely chopped, if available)
1 kg (2 lb) puff pastry (page 175)
yolk of 1 egg
1 dessertspoon milk
1 bunch of watercress for decoration

1 oven dish to take leg
1 pastry brush
1 pointed kitchen knife
1 paper frill for leg

Rub the leg of lamb with the garlic and the oil, scatter the salt and pepper over it and place in an oven dish with the carrot and sliced onion around it. Cook for 30 minutes in a moderate oven, 200 °C (400 °F)/Mark 6. Allow the leg to cool, then carve it in thin slices. Carefully put the slices back to re-form the leg.

Mix the sausagemeat, the mushrooms and the chopped onion together with the parsley and rosemary, add a little salt and pepper. Cover the leg with this mixture.

Roll out three-quarters of the pastry to about 30 × 40 cm (12 × 16 in). Place the leg of lamb in the centre, bring up the sides of the pastry and envelop the leg, leaving about a quarter uncovered. Wet the edges of the pastry. Roll out the remainder of the pastry and cut it in the shape of a pear. Place this 'cover' over the uncovered upper part of the leg. With the remainder of the pastry cut out little leaves and stick them round the 'cover', arranging them one slightly over the other. Brush the 'cover' with a glaze made from the egg and milk and then, if you wish, draw veins on the leaves and diagonal lines across the 'cover' in the shape of diamonds. Use the point of a small knife to do this. Allow the leg to stand for 20 minutes so that the pastry shrinks into position. Place in a baking dish in a preheated oven, 200 °C (400 °F)/Mark 6 for 20 minutes, then turn down to 150 °C (300 °F)/Mark 2 and continue cooking for another 15 minutes.

To serve, cut the pastry into diamonds or strips so that guests can help themselves more easily. Place the leg of lamb in a heated serving dish, add a frill round the bone if you wish and decorate with a bunch of fresh watercress.

For a sauce you can skim off the fat from the roasting pan and mix the pan juices with a little dry white wine, or serve the traditional mint sauce (page 124), mint and apple jelly (page 125), or redcurrant jelly.

Agneau de Lait à l'Oseille
Baby Lamb with Sorrel

The chef and I like this dish as it is light and elegant, an excellent example of modern French cuisine.

SERVES 8

100 g (3½ oz) butter
100 g (3½ oz) chopped onion
1 shoulder of baby lamb, about
    1.6 kg (3½ lb), boned and rolled
500 ml (1 pint) meat stock
1 *bouquet garni*
salt and pepper
250 g (9 oz) fresh double cream
50 g (1¾ oz) sorrel, finely
    chopped

1 heavy-bottomed casserole

Heat the butter in the casserole. Lightly fry the onion and remove from fat. Then fry the meat, turning it so that it is golden on all sides, add the stock, fried onion and the *bouquet garni*. Cover and cook gently for 30 minutes. Remove the *bouquet*, add the salt, pepper and cream. Cook for a further 10 minutes. Add the sorrel and allow to stand for 5 minutes before serving so that the taste is drawn out.

Serve in a deep dish surrounded by new potatoes boiled and tossed in butter and parsley.

Epaule d'Agneau Farcie à l'Anglaise
English Stuffed Shoulder of Lamb

This is an inexpensive, light dish, which we serve for lunches in the summer. We pass round a mint sauce, or sometimes a mint and apple jelly which is greatly appreciated (page 125), as well as the strained cooking juices.

SERVES 10

shoulder of lamb weighing
   1.6 kg (3½ lb)
450 g (1 lb) sausagemeat
50 g (1¾ oz) breadcrumbs mixed
   with a little milk
1 egg
80 g (2¾ oz) onion, chopped
1 soupspoon parsley, chopped
½ teaspoon crushed thyme
½ teaspoon rosemary powder
salt and pepper
100 g (3½ oz) butter
1 carrot, sliced
1 medium-sized onion, sliced

300 ml (½ pint) water

1 mixing bowl
string
1 cocotte or braising pan with lid

Bone the shoulder and open it out flat. Mix the sausagemeat, breadcrumbs, egg, chopped onion, parsley, thyme and rosemary in a mixing bowl. Add salt and pepper. Place this stuffing in the middle of the boned meat, roll and tie with string.

Melt the butter in the pan and toss the carrot, the sliced onion and the rolled shoulder in the butter. The shoulder should be well browned. Add the water and cook with the lid on in a preheated oven, 200 °C (400 °F)/Mark 6, for 1¼ hours. Pour off the cooking juices, skim off the fat, pass the juices through a fine strainer, heat and serve in a warmed sauceboat.

Cut the string, thinly slice the shoulder and decorate with a bunch of watercress and lightly boiled potatoes if you wish.

Pie de Mouton George V
George V's Mutton Pie

I do not know if George V ever ate this pie, and anyway the chef and I have adapted this traditional dish – and we like its name.

SERVES 8

1.6 kg (3½ lb) lean lamb or
  mutton
2 dessertspoons flour
150 g (5 oz) small white onions
100 g (3½ oz) butter
250 g (9 oz) carrots, sliced
1 *bouquet garni*
salt and pepper
1 litre (2 pints) meat stock
250 g (9 oz) peas
200 g (7 oz) apples, peeled, cored
  and diced
500 g (1 lb) pie dough
yolk of 1 egg
2 dessertspoons milk

1 heavy pan with lid
1 25-cm (10-in) pie dish
1 kitchen knife
1 pastry brush

Note: The chef uses the meat from the leg.

Cut the mutton or lamb into cubes about 3.5 cm (1½ in) square, removing all the fat. Dip the cubes in the flour, shake off all excess flour and toss until golden with the onions in the butter in a heavy pan. Add the carrots (the chef cuts them with a vegetable cutter and leaves them the size of a small olive) and the *bouquet garni*, salt, pepper and the meat stock. Cover and cook slowly for 40 minutes. Cool and add the peas and apples. Remove the *bouquet garni*.

Prepare a buttered pie dish by cutting a strip of pastry for the rim, wet the rim and press the pastry strip down firmly. Roll out the 'lid'. Fill the pie dish with the lamb mixture and cover with the pie crust. Decorate as you wish (with small leaves and a rosette and draw lines across with the tip of a knife). Use a pastry brush to glaze the crust with a mixture of the egg and milk. Place in a preheated very hot oven, 230 °C (450 °F)/Mark 8, for 10 minutes, then reduce to 190 °C (375 °F)/Mark 5 for 20 minutes. If the pastry is cooking too rapidly, cover it with foil paper. Before serving the chef cuts the lid into slices with kitchen scissors and serves the pie with a napkin tied round the base. He decorates his dish with a bunch of fresh watercress.

Contre-filet à l'Anglaise
English Roast Beef

You do not have to serve English food at a British Embassy. But in Paris where the choice of food is important for official occasions I like to serve a typical British dish to French officials, particularly because when it is cooked by a French chef it has great finesse. And there is nothing to compare with the Angus beef which we fly in from Scotland. As our kitchens are quite a distance from the dining room, we often use two beautiful meat trolleys. The two butlers serve the meat, and the footmen and two maids pass the vegetables, sauces, etc. It is a very elegant British way to serve a large number of guests.

SERVES 8

1.6 kg (3½ lb) strip loin
200 g (7 oz) pork fat or bacon
1 large white onion, sliced
1 carrot, sliced
2 dessertspoons vegetable oil
sprig of thyme
1 bayleaf
salt and pepper
450 ml (¾ pint) veal stock or
    water

1 sharp knife
string
1 baking dish
1 strainer

Trim the loin, draw a knife over the fat to mark it into diamonds and tie the pork fat round the sides where there is no fat. Tie the joint with string, but not too tightly. Place the onion, carrot, oil, thyme and bayleaf in the baking dish and arrange the meat over this. Bake in a very hot oven, 230 °C (450 °F)/Mark 8 for 15 minutes, then lower the temperature to 190 °C (375 °F)/Mark 5. Add salt and pepper, and continue to cook for 30 minutes, basting every 10 minutes. Untie, and leave the meat to stand for 15 minutes on an open oven door or in an open oven to keep it warm. Meanwhile pour off the fat from the baking dish, add the stock to the pan juices, cook for 15 minutes, check for salt and pepper and strain through a fine strainer. Slice the beef in very thin slices and arrange in the centre of a warmed serving dish, with a lightly cooked vegetable of your choice around it. We serve a horseradish sauce too (page 127) and sometimes a second vegetable – either spinach Barcelona (page 97) or brussels sprouts.

We always follow the tradition of serving Yorkshire pudding with the roast beef, which sometimes puzzles our French guests but is made deliciously light by our French pastry cook.

Yorkshire Pudding

MAKES ABOUT 25 INDIVIDUAL
PUDDINGS
3 eggs
200 g (7 oz) flour, sifted
400 ml (⅔ pint) milk

pinch nutmeg
salt to taste
white of 1 egg, beaten
300 ml (½ pint) vegetable oil

1 mixing bowl
patty tins or moulds, 6 cm (2½ in)
   in diameter by 2 cm (¾ in) high
absorbent paper

Mix all the ingredients except the oil and egg white in a mixing bowl and allow to stand for 2 hours. Add the beaten egg white to the batter and place the empty patty tins or moulds in a preheated very hot oven, 230 °C (450 °F)/Mark 8. When they are hot, drop 1 dessertspoon of vegetable oil into each mould. When the oil is hot, spoon 2 dessertspoons of the pudding mixture into each mould and put back into the oven for 10 minutes. Turn out on a piece of absorbent paper to remove excess grease. (You can use just one baking tin and cut the pudding into squares before serving if you prefer.)

The traditional way to cook Yorkshire pudding is to use dripping instead of vegetable oil but the chef's method is lighter and preferred by our French guests.

Filet de Boeuf Wellington
Fillet of Beef Wellington

This is a rather apt dish to serve in the British Embassy in Paris. It is, of course, a traditional international dish. Like our roast beef, we serve it with Angus beef from Scotland, and the wrapping is carefully done à la française by the chef.

SERVES 8

350 g (12 oz) mushrooms

50 g (1¾ oz) butter

400 g (14 oz) chicken livers or *foie gras*

1 truffle, weighing 40 g (1½ oz), chopped

2 kg (4½ lb) fillet of beef

1 kg (2 lb) puff pastry (page 175)

yolk of 1 egg

500 ml (scant pint) Madeira sauce (page 123)

1 medium-sized heavy-bottomed pan

1 sieve

1 ovenproof dish

1 pastry brush

1 sharp knife

Clean and dice the mushrooms, sauté them in butter, and drain. Sauté the livers in the same butter, then press them through a sieve to obtain a purée. Mix the mushrooms, livers and chopped truffle together.

Toss the fillet of beef in butter until it is golden on all sides. Allow it to cool. Roll out the pastry in a rectangle, cover the fillet with the mushroom-liver mixture and place it in the centre of the pastry. Seal the pastry round the fillet by wetting the edges. Place the fillet in the buttered baking dish, with the join underneath it. Glaze with the egg yolk and decorate as you wish with the point of a kitchen knife. Take care not to cut through the pastry.

Cook in a preheated moderate oven, 200 °C (400 °F)/Mark 6, for 30–40 minutes. Allow the fillet to stand 15 minutes before cutting it. The fillet continues to cook gently in the pastry while it stands. The chef serves a Madeira sauce with this.

You can decorate the dish with fresh watercress and serve it with baked potatoes or *pommes noisettes* (page 104). Braised lettuce, Spinach Barcelona or Brussels Sprouts Cavendish are also a good accompaniment (see chapter on vegetables).

Pie Pickwick
Pickwick Pie

This is a steak and kidney pie with oysters. The oysters should be added when the pie has been cooked and allowed to cool and is being heated up with the pie crust, as they become hard when overcooked. Cockles are sometimes preferred, but in either case do not put too much salt in the pie. We serve steak and kidney pie for large buffets in the winter and we serve Pickwick Pie for special occasions. It is a traditional British dish and when cooked by the French chef is extremely elegant.

SERVES 8

4 medium-sized onions, sliced
90 g (3 oz) butter (or 7 dessertspoons oil)
500 g (1 lb) calves' kidneys
1.5 kg (3½ lb) beefsteak cut into pieces about 3 cm (1¼ in) square
4 dessertspoons flour
salt and freshly-ground pepper
250 ml (½ pint) beef stock
pinch powdered clove
pinch marjoram
2 bayleaves
2 dessertspoons parsley, chopped
1 dessertspoon Worcestershire sauce
500 g (1 lb) mushrooms, lightly fried
18 oysters or cockles, shelled (optional)
500 g (1 lb) pie pastry (pages 175 and 178)
yolk of 1 egg
2 dessertspoons milk
150 ml (¼ pint) sherry

1 frying pan
1 bowl of salted water
1 heavy saucepan with lid
1 25-cm (10-in) oval pie dish
1 pastry brush

Fry the onions in butter or oil. Clean the kidneys and soak them in salted water for at least 1 hour. Slice kidneys and dice them. Dip steak and kidney pieces into the mixture of flour, salt and freshly-ground pepper and fry them in the fat used for the onions. Toss meat until golden, then pour in stock, add spices and herbs and simmer in a covered heavy saucepan for 1½ hours. Allow to cool. (All this can be done the day before if you wish.)

Place the cold cooked steak and kidneys with the cooking juices in the pie dish. Add the Worcestershire sauce and the mushrooms. Add the oysters or cockles at this point if you wish. If the cooking juices are too thin, add a little flour mixed with cold water. Check taste for salt and pepper. Invert an egg cup or pie funnel in the centre of the dish.

Roll out the pastry. Cut one strip and press this around the pie dish, having wetted the sides with cold water first. Then lift the pie crust with the rolling pin (see page 161) and place it on top of the dish. Wet your fingers with cold water and press down the pastry edges. Decorate the top with pieces of left-over dough, then brush the pastry with a glaze made from the egg yolk and milk. Make a hole in the centre to allow steam to escape and make a decoration which you can put over this hole when you serve the pie (cook this separately). Bake in a hot oven, 230–240 °C (450–475 °F)/Mark 8–9 for 10 minutes, then lower heat to a moderately hot oven 190–220 °C (375–425 °F)/Mark 5–7 and bake for 15–20 minutes. Just before serving, add the sherry through the funnel hole and cover with decoration.

If you have forgotten or do not like the idea of making a pastry decoration to cover the hole in the centre of the pie, tuck in a bunch of parsley or watercress instead. It looks just as elegant and is more original.

Veau Belgrade
Veal Belgrade

This is a dish I was served at the Hotel Metropol in Belgrade. The maître d'hôtel *kindly gave me the recipe and we often serve it for small lunch parties.*

SERVES 6

500 g (1 lb) spinach
500 g (1 lb) fresh green beans
6 small fillets of veal
juice of 1 lemon
3 dessertspoons olive oil
salt and freshly-ground black pepper
2 onions, chopped
3–4 green peppers, seeded and sliced
1 dessertspoon thyme or finely-chopped mixed herbs
3 eggs
1 dessertspoon parsley, chopped
½ teaspoon nutmeg, grated

1 large pan
1 strainer
1 medium-sized saucepan
1 medium-sized heavy-bottomed frying pan with lid
1 ovenproof dish

Wash the spinach and simmer wet for 5 minutes in a large covered pan. If the spinach is old, cook it in boiling water with a little salt for about 15 minutes. Drain well and chop into large pieces. Prepare the beans and cook them in boiling salted water for 10–15 minutes. Strain when still firm. Rub the meat with lemon juice and a little oil, then sprinkle with salt and freshly-ground pepper. Put under the grill and, when crisply cooked, slice into strips. Heat the olive oil, gently fry the onions and green peppers, cover and simmer for 20 minutes, then add and toss the green vegetables. Add the herbs and test seasoning.

About 25 minutes before serving, mix meat with vegetables and turn into an ovenproof dish. Beat the eggs with the parsley, grated nutmeg and a pinch of salt and pour over the dish. Place in a moderate oven 160 °C (325 °F)/Mark 3 for about 20 minutes or until the top is a golden colour.

Note: A good way to drain spinach is to put it back in the pan after draining it, with a little butter: shake the pan as it heats up and water evaporates.

It is important not to overcook the vegetables in this dish and to drain them well. You can use crisply grilled chicken or lamb instead of veal.

Cotelette de Veau St James
Veal Cutlets St James

This is a traditional English dish served with an original sauce chosen by the chef. The combination is very good and easy to cook.

SERVES 8

1 kg (2 lb) minced veal
150 g (5 oz) York ham, diced
150 g (5 oz) mushrooms, diced
150 g (5 oz) bacon, diced
peel of 1 orange, blanched and
   grated
salt and pepper to taste
200 g (7 oz) flour, sifted
1 egg
1 dessertspoon oil
250 g (9 oz) fresh breadcrumbs
150 g (5 oz) butter

1 mixing bowl
3 plates for flour, egg and
   breadcrumbs
1 frying pan

For the sauce:
2 shallots, chopped
50 g (1¾ oz) butter
200 ml (⅓ pint) dry white wine
200 ml (⅓ pint) concentrated meat
   stock
100 ml (scant ¼ pint) orange juice
1 teaspoon Colman's powdered
   mustard
1 teaspoon Worcestershire sauce
3 peppercorns, crushed

1 small heavy saucepan

Mix the veal, ham, mushrooms, bacon, orange rind, salt and pepper. Mould into little balls (about 16 of them, weighing about 90 g (3 oz) each) and flatten out into the shape of a cutlet with a 'bone'. Dip first in the flour, then in the egg beaten with the oil, and finally in the breadcrumbs. Fry the 'cutlets' in the butter gently for 3 minutes on each side.

To make the sauce, toss the shallots in the butter, add the wine and cook until it has lost half its volume. Add the stock, orange juice, mustard powder, Worcestershire sauce, crushed peppercorns (fresh green peppercorns are ideal for this), and salt. Simmer gently for 5 minutes.

Arrange the cutlets on a warm dish decorated with a bunch of fresh watercress or parsley, and serve the sauce separately.

Rouleaux de Veau aux Olives
Veal Rolls with Olives

My Spanish cook used to serve this when I was in Madrid, where we used Serrano ham. In Paris we use Parma ham. We have served it for lunch parties in the winter, sometimes followed by a ginger pudding (page 157) and the guests were delighted

SERVES 6–8
6 slices veal (escalopes)
6–8 slices Parma ham
10–15 black olives
3 onions, chopped and lightly fried
6 anchovy fillets
1 teaspoon chopped tarragon
grated rind of ½ orange
50–60 g (1¾–2 oz) flour
freshly-ground pepper and very little salt to taste
60 g (2 oz) butter
250 ml (½ pint) sherry or montilla

1 mixing bowl
toothpicks or string
1 heavy pan with lid

Flatten the slices of veal and cut them into two, trimming the edges. Cut the ham to fit the veal slices. Chop the olives and mix them with the onions, pounded anchovy fillets, tarragon and orange rind. Spread this mixture on the fillets, roll and fix them with a toothpick or tie with string. Dust them with seasoned flour and toss them in butter. When the fillets are golden, add the sherry or montilla, cover, and cook gently for 20 minutes. You can add cream to the sauce if you wish before serving. Decorate with chopped or whole tarragon leaves and some olives.

Pie de Veau Victoria
Victorian Veal Pie

This is a good pie to serve for a cold dinner or buffet. It is pretty and easy to make.

SERVES 8

500 ml (scant pint) jellied meat
    stock (page 173)
4 hard-boiled eggs, sliced
5 thin slices York ham
500 g (1 lb) lean veal, diced
400 g (14 oz) York ham, diced
about 15 whole parsley leaves
salt and pepper

1 25-cm (10-in) pie dish
1 mixing bowl
silver foil

Coat the pie dish with a little jellied stock. Carefully arrange the egg slices round it and line the dish with the slices of ham – the chef arranges them rather like a fan. Mix the diced meat and ham with the parsley leaves, season, and fill the dish. Pour over the remaining jellied meat stock. Cook gently in a preheated, moderately hot oven 190 °C (375 °F)/Mark 5 for 1½ hours, covered with a piece of silver foil. Allow to cool and keep in a refrigerator. Before serving dip the dish in boiling water, taking care not to allow water to reach the pie, and unmould on a prepared serving dish (the chef lies it on a bed of very finely chopped parsley).

Pie au Porc
Pork Pie

We serve this for small lunch or dinner parties when we do not know if and when guests will turn up. The pie keeps well in the refrigerator until it is needed. We serve it with a large bowl of salad. The chef uses decorative game pie moulds but you can use a cake tin with a removable rim if you wish. And the decoration is a matter of taste – the chef likes to use carefully cut-out leaves round the rim and a rosette in the centre. A large bunch of parsley or watercress and a few radishes make the pie even prettier.

SERVES 8
about 375 g (¾ lb) broken pork
    bones
salt and freshly-ground pepper
mixed herbs: thyme, rosemary,
    parsley and a bayleaf

Make some jellied pork stock by putting the bones in a large pan. Cover them with about 1.5 litres (3 pints) water, bring to the boil and add a little salt, pepper, herbs and the onion. Simmer for 3 hours at least, strain. (You can do this the day before you wish to cook the dish.)

1 large onion, quartered
1.5 kg (3½ lb) lean pork
1 teaspoon nutmeg, grated

1 large pan

For the paste:
500 g (1 lb 2 oz) flour
salt
170 g (6 oz) lard
125 ml (¼ pint) water

1–2 eggs, beaten

1 sieve
1 mixing bowl
1 small pan
1 22.5-cm (9-in) cake tin with
    removable base
1 pastry brush
greaseproof or foil paper

Dice the meat and leave it in a dish well sprinkled with salt, pepper and grated nutmeg. Meanwhile, make the hot water paste, which sounds difficult but is not *as long as you remember to keep paste warm throughout the operation.*

Sieve the flour and some salt into bowl. Bring lard to the boil in the water. Boil for 3 minutes, remove from fire and pour over flour. Mix rapidly and well, knead paste until smooth. Keep in a warm place.

Roll out a quarter of the paste to line the bottom of the greased tin, leaving the remainder in a warm place while you do this. Roll out half the remainder of the paste into wide strips to line the sides of the tin. Press these firmly against the sides, letting pastry project above the tin top. Brush all sides liberally with beaten egg. Put the meat into pie, add 5 dessertspoons of stock. Roll out remaining paste. Cut into a circle 2.5 cm (1 in) bigger than the top of the tin and use to cover the meat. Fold sides of pastry over the pastry lid like a hem and pinch together for decoration. Cut small slits in the centre, decorate with pastry leaves and brush copiously with beaten egg.

Bake for 1 hour in a moderately hot oven 180 °C (350 °F)/Mark 4, then cover with several layers of greaseproof paper or foil paper and cook for a further 2 hours in a cooler oven, 160 °C (325 °F)/Mark 3. When the pie is cooked. pour the jellied stock into it through the slits. Leave overnight to set. Serve cold decorated with parsley.

You can also use this method for veal and ham pie. Use three-quarters the amount of veal, one-quarter of ham or gammon. Dice veal, cut ham into strips.

Jambon Glacé au Caramel
Sugar-Glazed Ham

This is a traditional American dish but greatly appreciated in Paris. The chef serves it hot or cold. With the hot ham he serves a Sauce Madère – *Madeira sauce; with the cold ham he serves a Cumberland sauce (pages 123 and 122).*

SERVES 10

1 York or Prague ham, weighing
   3 kg (6 lb)
20 g ($\frac{3}{4}$ oz) cloves
250 ml (scant $\frac{1}{2}$ pint) Madeira
250 g (9 oz) brown sugar

1 large pan of cold water
1 sharp knife
1 large braising dish with lid

Prepare and cook your ham as on page 79 but remove it from the heat half an hour earlier, after 1$\frac{1}{2}$ hours, before it is completely cooked. Skin the ham, leaving a 'frill' of 7.5 cm (3 in) at the end of the bone which you serrate with a sharp knife for decoration. Insert the cloves into the fat all over the ham. (For a more decorative dish you should insert them in diagonal lines so that diamonds are formed.) Put the ham in a braising dish with the Madeira. Cover the dish with a lid and place in a very cool oven, 100 °C (220 °F)/Mark $\frac{1}{4}$ for 1 hour. Then add the sugar to the cooking juices, baste, and continue cooking until the sugar has become caramelized. Slice hot or cold with a very sharp carving knive and put the meat back on the bone. The chef puts a frill on the bone for decoration.

Jambon de York au Parmesan
York Ham with Parmesan Cheese

This is a change from the traditional way of serving roast ham. The Parmesan cheese and, if you have time, the home-made noodles lend a delicious Italian flavour. Our recipe adds a French touch in the way it is cooked and served.

SERVES 10

1 York ham on the bone, weighing 3 kg (6 lb)
450 g (1 lb) Parmesan cheese, grated
500 ml (scant pint) béchamel sauce (page 121)
300 g (11 oz) fresh breadcrumbs
4–5 eggs
100 g (4 oz) butter, melted
300 g (11 oz) fresh cream

1 large pot
1 sharp knife
1 large baking dish
kitchen scissors

Soak the ham in a large pot of cold water, changing the water every hour or so for 6 hours to remove salt. During this time you can clean the ham, scrubbing it with a hard brush. Cut the tip off the bone and scrape the skin off a little way down, making a kind of 'handle'. (In the UK the other bone at the chump end of the ham is normally removed before you buy it. However, if this has not been done you should remove it.)

To cook the ham, place it in a large pot of cold water and bring to the boil. Then lower heat so that the pot barely simmers for 2 hours. Meanwhile mix 150 g (5 oz) Parmesan with half the béchamel. When the ham is cooked, take it out of the water and remove all the skin, leaving just a ring for decoration round the bone and serrating the edge with a pointed knife if you wish. Thinly slice the ham, then put the slices back on the bone to re-form the ham, spreading a layer of béchamel and Parmesan mixture between each slice. Mix 200 g (7 oz) of the remaining Parmesan with the breadcrumbs and the eggs and coat the ham with this mixture. Place the ham in a buttered baking dish and cook in a preheated moderate oven, 200 °C (400 °F)/Mark 6, for 5 minutes, or until the cover mixture dries out. Then baste with the melted butter and return to the oven for ½ hour. If you want a really golden cover, baste every 5 minutes; if the ham is cooking too fast, cover with foil.

When the ham is cooked, cut the cover with a sharp knife or with kitchen scissors in strips or diamonds to make serving easier. Serve with a frill and a bunch of watercress if you wish. We serve it with fresh, lightly cooked peas in heaps dotted over home-made noodles (page 106).

To make the sauce to go with this dish, bring to the boil the remaining béchamel, the fresh cream and 100 g (4 oz) Parmesan. Serve in sauceboat.

Moussaka

This is a family recipe and I must admit we have not been very generous about letting our friends have it. My daughter Alexandra was furious when she heard it was to be published. The chef serves moussaka for large buffets and for small informal lunches; it is always appreciated.

SERVES 6–8

3 onions, chopped

2 dessertspoons butter or 3 dessertspoons olive oil

750 g (1½ lb) mixed minced lamb, beef or veal (I mix lamb and beef)

1 cup dry white wine

2 dessertspoons tomato purée

salt and pepper

3 dessertspoons fresh, chopped herbs (preferably parsley and thyme)

250 ml (scant ½ pint) oil or melted butter for frying

750 g (1½ lb) tomatoes

750 g (1½ lb) courgettes

750 g (1½ lb) aubergines

2 dessertspoons flour

7 dessertspoons breadcrumbs

whites of 2 eggs, stiffly beaten

2 dessertspoons chopped parsley

2 large frying pans, 1 with lid

1 ovenproof dish

For the béchamel:

3 dessertspoons butter

6 dessertspoons flour

3 cups hot milk

3 dessertspoons cheese, grated

1 teaspoon nutmeg, grated

yolks of 2 eggs

1 heavy-bottomed saucepan

Fry the onions in butter or oil and then add the meat and lightly brown it. Add the wine, tomato purée, salt, pepper and herbs. Cover and simmer for 1 hour. Meanwhile slice and fry the vegetables using the 250 ml (scant ½ pint) oil or butter. I prefer vegetable oil but the original recipe uses olive oil. If any one of the vegetables is not available, use 750 g (1½ lb) peeled and sliced potatoes instead. Dip tomatoes and courgettes into flour before frying. When all the vegetables are lightly fried, prepare an ovenproof dish. Grease it and scatter some breadcrumbs on the bottom and sides of the dish. When the meat is cooked, remove from fire and stir in the remainder of the breadcrumbs and the beaten egg whites. Place a layer of aubergines at the bottom of the dish and then a layer of the meat mixture. Continue placing layers of vegetables and meat alternately, sprinkling a little salt, pepper and parsley over each layer until the dish is full.

Make a stiff béchamel by heating the butter and when melted add the flour and stir. Add the hot milk all at once and bring to the boil. Remove from the fire and stir briskly. Add salt, pepper, cheese and grated nutmeg. Re-heat and then remove from fire and add the egg yolks one at a time, beating briskly. Pour the béchamel over the meat and vegetable mixture and place dish in a very slow oven 140 °C (275 °F)/Mark 1 for 1 hour. Remove 10 minutes before serving. Cut into slices to make serving easier. For buffets we cut criss-cross in diamond shapes. Decorate with a bunch of parsley if you wish.

Keftedes: Boules de Viande Grecques
Keftedes: Greek Meat Balls

These meat balls are excellent for cocktail parties, delicious for picnics, and also make a good light lunch or dinner dish when made larger and served hot with potato purée or cold with mayonnaise and potato salad. The same mixture can be used for hamburgers, grilled and served in slit, round, buttered rolls. We have done the latter for teenage Embassy parties.

SERVES 6

750 g (1½ lb) minced beef and veal, mixed (or beef and lamb)

250 g (½ lb) bacon, minced

2 thick slices crustless white bread, soaked in cold water

5 dessertspoons parsley, chopped

1½ dessertspoons thyme, chopped (or mint or marjoram)

4 dessertspoons breadcrumbs

3 onions: 2 chopped and lightly fried, 1 just chopped

3 dessertspoons flour

salt and pepper

2 eggs

115 g (4 oz) flour for rolling

250 ml (scant ½ pint) oil for frying

1 deep mixing bowl
1 plate
1 deep frying pan
absorbent paper

Put the minced meat, bacon, bread (squeeze out the water first, and break the bread into pieces), parsley, thyme, breadcrumbs and onions in a bowl. Mix well. Sprinkle over the flour, salt and pepper to taste and mix again. Add the eggs and mix well. Then take a heaped teaspoon of the mixture, roll it into a ball, roll this in some flour on a plate and stand it on a piece of kitchen paper. Continue the process until all the mixture is used. (You will need about 115 g (4 oz) flour.) Heat the oil and fry the meat balls over a medium heat until golden. Remove and drain fat by standing balls on a piece of absorbent paper. Place in a warm serving dish and serve hot or cold.

Chou Farci Limousine
Stuffed Cabbage Limousine

This is an original dish and looks amusing. It tastes delicious but I must admit needs some time to prepare. It is ideal for a small dinner party and is always praised when it is served.

SERVES 6
1 large cabbage
200 g (7 oz) chestnuts
1 litre (2 pints) meat stock
30 g (1 oz) fresh breadcrumbs
40 g (1½ oz) onions, chopped
500 g (1 lb) sausagemeat
salt and pepper
1 dessertspoon parsley, chopped
100 g (3½ oz) strips of fat (or
   unsmoked bacon)
8 slices bacon
1 dessertspoon tomato purée
1 dessertspoon cornflour
100 ml (⅕ pint) Madeira

1 pan to boil cabbage
1 saucepan
1 mixing bowl
string
1 heavy cocotte or casserole

Cook the cabbage for 10 minutes in boiling salted water, then drain. Carefully remove the cabbage leaves and lie them one on top of the other. When you get to the heart, remove it.

Peel the chestnuts and cook them for 10 minutes in the meat stock. Drain, and keep the stock. Make a mixture with the breadcrumbs, onions, sausagemeat, chestnuts, salt, pepper and parsley. Make a small ball with some of the mixture and put it in the centre of the cabbage (where you have removed the heart). Cover it with a few cabbage leaves, coat these with the sausage mixture and continue to re-make your cabbage, spreading a layer of the stuffing between each layer of leaves. When you have re-made the cabbage, lie the strips of fat horizontally right round the base of the cabbage and place the bacon slices vertically, stretching downwards from the top of the cabbage to the ring of fat strips. Tie the whole cabbage securely with kitchen string rather like a parcel, so as to keep the leaves and the strips of bacon in place. Put the cabbage in a cocotte or casserole. Pour over the stock which was used to cook the chestnuts so that it reaches halfway up the cabbage. Add the tomato purée and the cornflour diluted in the Madeira.

Place the tightly covered pan in a slow oven, 150 °C (300 °F)/Mark 2, for 3 hours. Baste very often during the cooking time. You may have to add a little more stock. The cabbage should be well glazed and the juices well concentrated.

Untie the cabbage – it will remain intact – and serve in a dish with a circle of freshly boiled potatoes with a little parsley. Serve the juices separately in a sauceboat.

Timbale de Macaroni au Poulet
Chicken and Macaroni Pie

This is a wonderful dish for a one-course lunch, served with a fresh green salad. We have often used it, too, for a surprise picnic dish. We wrap it up in foil and try to keep it warm. It is then tied up in a cloth – peasant-style. When unwrapped, it never fails to please our guests. The chef often likes to make two smaller pies using game pie moulds – they are prettier.

SERVES 8

250 g (9 oz) lean bacon, diced
70 g (5 dessertspoons) tomato paste
60 g (2 oz) butter
3 medium-sized onions, chopped
2 soupspoons peanut or similar vegetable oil for frying
1 chicken, about 1.6 kg (3½ lb) cut up in pieces
250 g (9 oz) mushrooms, chopped and lightly fried in oil
250 ml (scant ½ pint) dry white wine
250 g (9 oz) sausages (pork chipolatas or frankfurters)
250 g (9 oz) macaroni

1 medium-sized pan
1 heavy pan with lid
1 frying pan
1 large pan

For the béchamel:
30 g (1 oz) butter
30 g (1 oz) flour, sieved
250 ml (½ pint) milk, warmed
80 g (2¾ oz) grated cheese (fresh Parmesan or mature Cheddar)
salt and pepper

1 small heavy pan
1 whisk

Prepare the bacon by cooking it in about 2 litres (4 pints) boiling water for 3 minutes, then drain. To give the tomato paste a sweeter taste, cook it in 30 g (1 oz) butter for about 5 minutes. Fry the onions in another 30 g (1 oz) butter mixed with the oil until they are transparent and golden. Add the chicken pieces, bacon, mushrooms and tomato paste. Pour in the wine and simmer in covered pan for about 30 minutes. Remove the chicken, bone and dice. Fry the sausages gently, then chop. Cook the macaroni in a large pan of boiling, salted water – 8 g (1½ teaspoons) salt for 1 litre (2 pints) water. Cook for 8–10 minutes and strain. Pour cold water over the macaroni and drain.

Make a béchamel sauce by melting the butter. When it becomes frothy, add the flour and beat with a whisk. Add the warm milk all at once and stir so that there are no lumps. Beat and add the grated cheese, salt and pepper.

Put the drained macaroni in a large mixing bowl, add the chicken pieces, the chopped sausages, bacon, mushrooms, parsley, thyme and the tepid béchamel sauce and mix well. Taste for seasoning and add more salt and pepper as required.

Butter the pie mould. Roll out the pastry in two pieces. Make one the shape of the mould so that it will cover the base and sides of the mould all in one piece, allowing it to overlap by 2.5 cm (1 in). Make the other (to be used as a lid) about 2.5 cm (1 in) larger than the base of the mould. When you have lined the mould, paint the base with the lightly beaten egg white, using a pastry brush. This prevents the pastry from becoming soggy. Fill the mould with the chicken and macaroni mixture.

1 soupspoon parsley, chopped
1 teaspoon thyme, chopped

1 large earthenware mixing bowl

For the pie crust:
600 g (1¼ lb) pie dough (page 178)
1 egg, separated
1 soupspoon milk

1 round pie mould or cake tin,
    22.5 cm (9 in) in diameter
1 pastry brush

Brush the edges of the mould with the remainder of the egg white mixed with a little water. Cover the filled mould with the pastry lid and pinch the edges with your fingers or a knife all the way round. With any remains of the pastry, cut out some leaves, decorating them (putting in veins, etc.) with a knife. Decorate the top of the pie with these. Make a hole in the centre to allow the steam to escape and not spoil the crisp pie crust. Paint the top of the pie with the egg yolk mixed with the milk. Cook in a moderate oven, 200 °C (400 °F)/Mark 6, for 1 hour. Remove, unmould and allow to stand before serving. This makes the cutting easier. Decorate with a bunch of fresh watercress or parsley if you wish.

Poulet à la Chilienne
Chilean Chicken Pie (Pastel de Choclo)

This is an excellent dish for a large party as it can be prepared well in advance – it is even better that way. I picked up the recipe when I was in Chile, and I now serve it in a large copper pan which was given to me when I was in Santiago. The chef likes using copper pans for hot dishes served on a buffet.

SERVES 6–8
1 large chicken or 2 small ones,
    cut into 8 pieces
3 dessertspoons butter or oil

1 large frying pan

For the Pino (meat mixture):
2 onions, sliced
500 g (1 lb) minced beef
1 sweet pepper, chopped (or one
    Chilean pepper, chopped)
2 dessertspoons herbs, finely
    chopped
½ dessertspoon paprika
salt and pepper
2 hard-boiled eggs, sliced
3 dessertspoons sultanas

Fry the chicken in half the butter or oil until golden, then remove from pan. In the same pan use the remaining butter or oil to fry the onion, adding the minced meat, sweet pepper, herbs, paprika and salt and pepper. Simmer all these ingredients until almost cooked. (*Note:* For the herbs in the *pino* Chileans use oregano or wild marjoram and cumin seed, which give the pie a special flavour. You can also use either chopped thyme and parsley or crushed rosemary or coriander seeds. The quantity depends on personal taste.)

Line the bottom of the pie dish or pan that you will use for serving the dish with the minced meat mixture. Arrange a layer of thin slices of hard-boiled eggs over this. Sprinkle with the sultanas and then place the chicken joints on top.

Meanwhile, prepare the corn mixture. Grate the cobs or mince the corn and simmer gently with 1 dessertspoon of butter and

1 large buttered ovenproof dish or copper pan which can be brought to the table

For the Choclo (corn mixture):
6–8 large corn cobs or 4 packets of frozen corn (about 500 g (1 lb))
2½ dessertspoons butter
125 ml (¼ pint) milk
1½ dessertspoons basil, chopped (or parsley and mint, mixed)
1½ dessertspoons castor sugar
2 teaspoons icing sugar

1 medium-sized heavy pan
1 grater or mincer

the milk. The quantity of milk depends on the type of corn: your finished corn mixture should look like a corn purée with the milk having been completely absorbed. Add the basil, castor sugar and salt to taste. When the *choclo* is half cooked (it will still be firm), pour it over the pie and dot with small pieces of the remaining butter. Sprinkle the icing sugar over the pie and bake in a moderate oven, 200 °C (400 °F)/Mark 6, for 40 minutes; the top should be a golden colour. (The addition of the butter and icing sugar can be done just before serving – the rest can be prepared in advance.)

You can use more corn and more chicken. For a large buffet, it is a good idea to have several layers of corn and chicken in a very large copper pan.

Canard aux Pêches
Duck with Peaches

I like duck to be crisp. That is not, however, the way it is usually served in France. And then I get a little tired of duck with oranges, so this is our favourite recipe. In Paris we use a special roasting duck called a canard Rouennais.

SERVES 4–6
1 duck, weighing about 2.5 kg (5 lb)
salt and pepper
1 tablespoon flour
90 g (3 oz) butter
6–8 peach halves, fresh or tinned, poached in butter
1 onion, sliced
250 g (9 oz) mushrooms, sliced
250 ml (scant ½ pint) red wine
2 teaspoons corn starch
chopped parsley for decoration

1 roasting tin
1 greased ovenproof serving dish
greaseproof paper or foil
1 heavy pan for the sauce

Rub the duck with salt and pepper, scatter a little flour over it and dot with some of the butter. Roast in a moderate oven, 160 °C (325 °F)/Mark 3, for 40 minutes, basting frequently. Allow the bird to cool a little, then bone. First remove bones from legs and dice the meat. Then carefully remove the breast and cut it into strips, and finally dice the remaining pieces of meat. Be sure to keep all the bones and the cooking juices in the pan.

Place the diced meat at the bottom of the ovenproof serving dish, laying it out in the shape of a duck. If you have the duck's drumsticks, put them back in position. Place some of the peaches over the diced meat and cover with the strips. Decorate the sides of the dish with the remaining peaches. Tuck knobs of butter under the strips of duck breast and dot the top with butter. Cover with foil or greaseproof paper and keep warm in low oven while you make the sauce.

Break up the bones and the carcass and put them in a pan with the onion, mushrooms and wine. Boil rapidly for 5 minutes, then add 500 ml (scant pint) water and simmer for 30 minutes. Strain.

Deglaze (in French, *déglacer*) the pan in which the duck was roasted by pouring off the fat, adding 2 teaspoons of corn starch, stirring and pouring in the wine sauce. Simmer for about 5 minutes, scraping the pan so that all the cooking juices mix with the sauce. Strain and serve in a sauceboat to accompany the duck.

You can serve the duck surrounded by a bed of lightly-cooked fresh peas (cooked in boiling water with fresh mint) and you can add sliced, lightly-fried mushrooms. Scatter chopped parsley over the duck but do not pour sauce over it as the duck would lose its crispness. We serve a white rice Cantonnais with this dish (page 107). You can serve a white rice with toasted almonds scattered over it too.

Pie de Dinde
Turkey Pie

We serve several of these pies at large buffets. They are more original than the usual buffet food. They can be made in advance and have the advantage of being a hot course for a large number of guests. The entrée or first course and the sweet can then be cold. The recipe is also an excellent way to use up cooked turkey over the Christmas holidays. If you do that, the cooking time given below must be reduced to 30–40 minutes,

SERVES 8
1.6 kg (3½ lb) boned turkey
100 g (3½ oz) butter
100 g (3½ oz) small white onions, peeled
100 g (3½ oz) carrots, sliced
200 g (7 oz) bacon, diced
100 g (3½ oz) mushrooms, peeled and halved if large

Slice the turkey breast into thick strips or *julienne* and blanch for 4 minutes. Dice the rest of the turkey meat and toss it in the butter with the onions, carrots, bacon, mushrooms and thyme. Add salt and pepper, then add the flour, shake, and stir and cook for about 2 minutes. Remove from the fire and allow to cool.

Prepare a pie dish (page 161). Roll out the pastry and wet the rim of the pie dish with cold water. Cut off a strip of the pastry to fit the rim of the dish and press down. Fill the pie dish with

1 teaspoon thyme
salt and freshly-ground pepper
50 g (1¾ oz) flour, sifted
500 g (1 lb) pastry (page 178)
450 ml (¾ pint) stock from the
    turkey bones and giblets
yolk of 1 egg
2 dessertspoons milk
150 ml (¼ pint) Madeira

1 small pan of boiling water for
    blanching
1 heavy frying pan or thick sauté
    pan
1 25-cm (10-in) oval pie dish
1 pie funnel or egg cup
1 pastry brush

the turkey mixture and add the stock. Put a pie funnel or an upturned egg cup in the centre. Cover the pie with the rest of the pastry, press down and pinch the edges. Cut a hole in the centre of the pie crust to allow the steam to escape. Decorate the pie with leaves cut out of the remains of the pastry and cut out a rosette to fill the hole when the pie is cooked, and cook this separately. Brush the pie with a glaze made from the egg and milk. (You can decorate the crust further by drawing lines with the tip of a knife across the pastry to form diamonds, if you wish.) Place the pie in a preheated moderately hot oven, 190 °C (375 °F)/Mark 5, for 1½ hours. If the pastry is cooking too quickly, cover with silver foil. Five minutes before removing the pie from the oven, pour in the Madeira through the hole in the crust. To serve, cut slices in the pie crust with kitchen scissors. Cover the hole with the pastry decoration or tuck in a bunch of parsley or watercress. Serve with a napkin round the dish to prevent slipping.

Pie de Gibier en Croûte
Game Pie

This is a traditional British dish and is very popular with our French guests. The pies – sometimes 6 or 8 of them served with folded, starched napkins round the basins and resting on beautiful Wellington silver trays — are a great attraction. They are delicious, too. Other game can be used if partridge is not available.

SERVES 8
2 partridges
75 g (2½ oz) butter
1 onion
2 leeks
2 carrots
salt and freshly-ground pepper
250 g (½ lb) bacon
250 g (½ lb) lean veal
250 g (½ lb) ham or pork

Chop the birds into neat joints. Remove as many bones as possible. Lightly fry the joints in butter. Put the bones in a saucepan with water, the onion, leeks, carrots and salt and pepper and boil to make stock. (You need about 700 ml (1¼ pints).) Line a pie dish with bacon and mince the rest of the bacon, the veal, the ham and the livers. Put all these ingredients in a basin and mix with shallots, herbs, orange rind, some salt and pepper and the spices. Add the breadcrumbs and the whole egg. Mix well; if it is too dry, add a little stock. Make into small forcemeat balls, roll these in a little flour and fry them lightly in butter.

250 g (½ lb) game and chicken
  livers
2 dessertspoons shallots, chopped
  and lightly fried
1 teaspoon thyme, chopped
1 teaspoon tarragon, chopped
grated rind of ½ orange
½ teaspoon powdered cloves
½ teaspoon nutmeg, grated
60 g (2oz) breadcrumbs
1 egg
115 g (4 oz) flour, sifted
3 dessertspoons parsley, chopped
2 hard-boiled eggs
250 g (½ lb) mushrooms, chopped
  and lightly fried
100 ml (⅛ pint) Madeira or sherry
500 g (1 lb) pastry dough (pages
  175 and 178)
yolk of 1 egg
2 dessertspoons milk

1 frying pan
1 saucepan for stock
1 deep 27-cm (10½-in) oval pie
  dish
1 mixing bowl
1 plate for flour
1 pie funnel or egg cup
1 pastry brush

Fill the pie dish by arranging a layer of game joints over the bacon sprinkled with salt and freshly-ground pepper and chopped parsley, then a layer of hard-boiled egg slices. On top of this add a layer of chopped mushrooms and over this the forcemeat balls. Repeat the layers until the pie is full. Then pour over some of the stock and Madeira (enough to fill the dish about three-quarters full). Invert an egg cup or place a pie funnel in the centre of the dish.

Cover with your favourite pastry, leaving a hole in the centre. (For pie cover, see page 161.) Brush with a glaze made from the egg yolk and milk and cook in a hot oven, 230 °C (450 °F)/Mark 8, for 10 minutes, then reduce to 190 °C (375 °F)/Mark 5 for 1½ hours. Before serving pour a little stock and a little Madeira through the hole in the centre of the pie. The chef and I prefer to cook the game pie (covered) without the crust for about ¾–1 hour so that one can arrange the pieces of game on top of the pie and see that the necessary amount of stock and Madeira is added. The crust can then be placed on the dish and the pie cooked in a hot oven, 230 °C (450 °F)/Mark 8, for 15–20 minutes until the crust is a rich golden colour.

To serve, you can arrange a bird's head in the centre hole for decoration and put a frill of parsley round its neck, but I prefer just a large bunch of watercress or parsley. The chef likes to cut the crust into slices before serving the pie as it makes it easier for guests – he also likes to peep inside to see that all is well. He puts back the sliced crust carefully and decorates the centre with a pastry rosette cooked separately.

Note: If you are cooking the pie without the crust, leave until cold before covering with pastry dough.

  If you do not wish to make forcemeat balls, you can spread the forcemeat mixture over the game joints in layers.

Pie de Pigeon
Pigeon Pie

This is an old English recipe and an amusing and unusual way to serve pigeons. It has been much appreciated by our French guests.

SERVES 8

1 onion, sliced
20 slices bacon, cut in half
8 pigeons, halved and boned if you wish
16 thin slices steak, cut into pieces 6 cm (2½ in) square
3 dessertspoons flour, sifted
400 g (14 oz) mushrooms, peeled, halved and quartered if large
1 litre (2 pints) chicken stock
pinch rosemary powder (or teaspoon crushed fresh rosemary)
2 crushed cloves (or a pinch clove powder)
salt and pepper
1 *bouquet garni* (thyme, bay, parsley)
150 ml (¼ pint) port
500 g (1 lb) pie pastry (page 178)
yolk of 1 egg
2 dessertspoons milk

1 heavy frying pan
1 25-cm (10-in) oval pie dish
silver foil
1 pastry brush

Lightly toss the onion and bacon together and then remove, leaving the fat in the pan. Toss the pigeon pieces in this fat, then dip the steaks in the flour, shake off any excess and toss these, too (adding a little fat if necessary).

Grease the pie dish with lard, and then fill it as follows. On the bottom of the dish arrange a layer of the bacon and onion mixture, then a layer of steak slices, then the pigeons, then mushrooms. Repeat these layers ending with the mushrooms. Cover with the stock and add the herbs and spices and *bouquet garni*. (Use stock cubes if you wish, to which you can add the pigeon bones, necks and giblets.) Cover with silver foil and cook in a preheated oven, 190 °C (375 °F)/Mark 5, for 1 hour. Remove the *bouquet garni* and allow to cool. Add the port.

Prepare the pie crust (page 161). Wet the edge of the pie dish and arrange a strip of the pastry round this. Press down firmly. Cut the 'lid' and cover the pie, pinching the edges so that they are well sealed. Dip your fingers in cold water first. Use a pastry brush to apply a glaze made from the egg yolk and milk. Decorate as you wish with diamonds drawn with the tip of a knife. (The chef lays a row of pastry leaves round the edge, glazes them and marks out the veins. He adds a rosette in the middle.) Place in a very hot preheated oven, 230 °C (450 °F)/Mark 8, for 10 minutes, then reduce to 190 °C (375 °F)/Mark 5 for 25 minutes, taking care that the pastry does not overcook. Cover with foil if necessary. To serve, cut slices in the pie with scissors if you wish – the chef does this to make serving easier – and fold a napkin round the dish. Decorate with fresh parsley.

Pie de Cailles
Quail Pie

I first had this dish at the Prefecture in Colmar and I thought it was delicious. I then discussed it with the chef and we adapted it and served it to the Queen Mother when she came in October 1976. Since then we have served Quail Pie when we wanted something light and special.

SERVES 5
2 kg (4½ lb) cooking apples
300 g (10½ oz) raisins
200 g (7 oz) butter
salt and pepper
½–1 teaspoon cinnamon
10 quails
200 ml (⅓ pint) Cognac
500 g (1 lb) shortcrust or puff
   pastry (pages 178 and 175)
200 ml (⅓ pint) Madeira
yolk of 1 egg
1 teaspoon milk
500 ml (generous ¾ pint) chicken
   stock
1 dessertspoon cornflour

2 medium-sized pans
1 large frying pan
string
1 40-cm (16-in) oval pie dish
1 sharp knife
1 pastry brush
1 fine-meshed strainer

Peel and quarter the apples and remove the pips. Cut the apples into small pieces and fry them gently with the raisins in half the butter until they are golden. Add salt, pepper and cinnamon and leave to get cold.

Clean and bone the quails. Fill them with the apple and raisin mixture and tie them up with string. Add salt and pepper and fry in the remainder of the butter. Pour over the Cognac and set alight or *flamber*. Cut the string and allow to cool.

Roll out the pastry until it is about 3 mm (⅛ in) thick. Cut a strip and press this round the edge of the oval pie dish (see drawing on page 161). Allow it to overlap the edge by 1 cm (½ in) or so. Place the quails in the pie dish, cover with the remainder of the apple and raisin mixture and pour over half the Madeira. Cut the pastry in the shape of the pie but about 1 cm (½ in) larger. Lift this over the pie and press down around the rim, securing it with a little water. Trim the pastry round the pie with a knife and press around the rim with your fingers.

Add decorative leaves cut out of the pastry scraps with a knife. Use a pastry brush to cover the top of the pie with the egg yolk mixed with the milk. Make a few holes in the pastry with a fork or sharp knife so that the steam can escape. You can, if you prefer, leave a hole in the centre of the pie and cover it later with a pastry rosette cooked separately. Allow the pie to stand for 15 minutes, then place in preheated moderate oven, 200 °C (400 °F)/Mark 6, for 15 minutes. Cover with foil and cook for 40 minutes more.

While the pie is cooking, fry the bones and giblets in the same pan in which you fried the quails. Pour over the chicken stock mixed with the cornflour. Cook for 20 minutes, check seasoning, strain and add the remaining Madeira to the sauce.

Before serving, remove the lid and pour a quarter of the sauce into the pie. Carefully divide the pie lid in slices. This helps the guests to serve themselves. Place it in an open, low oven to become crisp, then replace the lid before serving. Pour remainder of the sauce into a sauceboat. Place the pie dish on a serving dish with a folded napkin under it to prevent it from slipping. You can add a bunch of watercress for decoration.

Terrine de Marcassin
Young Wild Boar Terrine

This has been a very successful terrine for a grand buffet. We served it at a special Scottish dinner and it met with great approval.

SERVES 8

200 g (7 oz) veal fillet or best end neck
250 g (9 oz) lean, young boar meat
200 ml (scant ½ pint) brandy
salt and freshly-ground pepper
400 g (14 oz) pork throat
100 g (3½ oz) pistachio nuts, shelled
20 g (¾ oz) onion, chopped
200 g (7 oz) fresh pork fat (or fat bacon)
100 g (3½ oz) flour
500 ml (scant pint) jellied meat stock (page 173)
2 teaspoons Madeira
1 teaspoon parsley, chopped

1 mixing bowl
1 pan of boiling water
1 terrine, about 20 cm (8 in) long
1 baking pan
greaseproof paper

Choose a lean cut of veal; in France we would use the top round or *noix*. 'Pork throat' is a very fatty part of the pig. If unobtainable, choose a fatty cut.

Trim the veal and the wild boar (removing sinews and filaments) and dice. Marinate in the brandy, salt and pepper overnight. Mince the pork throat. Drop the pistachio nuts into boiling water and skin. Mix the nuts with the minced pork throat, the veal and the wild boar meat, the marinating juices, the chopped onion, and some salt and pepper. Blanch the fresh pork fat or bacon for 10 minutes and use it to line the terrine. Fill it with the meat mixture – in French, *la farce* – and cover the terrine with a lid. Hermetically seal the terrine by mixing the flour with a little water and rolling it out into a thick strip which you press down on the rim of the lid and on to the terrine's rim (see drawing). Place the terrine in a pan with water to come three-quarters up the side of the dish and cook in a preheated slow oven, 150 °C (300 °F)/Mark 2, for 1¼ hours. Remove the lid and place a weight covered with greaseproof paper on the terrine. When the terrine is cold (it will have shrunk), fill it with the jellied stock, mixed with the Madeira. This brings the fat to the surface. Skim and remove this, add a little more jellied stock which you mix with a little chopped parsley. Serve cold but not iced.

Lapin Sauté au Cidre
Sauté Rabbit with Cider

This is a light French dish for lunch. The chef likes to serve it with fresh noodles (page 106).

SERVES 8
100 g (3½ oz) butter
2 kg (4½ lb) rabbit, cut in pieces
3 shallots, chopped
30 g (1 oz) flour
1 litre (2 pints) good apple cider
salt and pepper
1 *bouquet garni* (sprig of parsley, chives, bayleaf, rosemary)
300 g (11 oz) fresh cream
2–3 apples, quartered
chopped parsley

1 heavy stewing pan with lid

Heat the butter in a heavy stewing pan and toss the rabbit pieces and shallots in it. Scatter the flour over the pieces and continue to fry until a golden colour. Then add the cider, salt (not too much to begin with; you can always correct the seasoning later), pepper and *bouquet garni*. Add a little water so that the rabbit pieces are well covered. Cook gently with the lid on for 1½ hours. Remove the rabbit pieces, throw away the *bouquet garni* and reduce the cooking juices by about half. (This will increase the saltiness of the sauce.) Add the cream to the reduced juices, then cook the rabbit pieces in this sauce for 5 minutes. Serve in a deep dish with apples lightly fried in butter and scatter chopped parsley over the whole dish.

Râble de Lapin Dijonnais
Rabbit Back Dijonnais

This is a sharp, fresh and very French dish. It makes an excellent lunch dish. Rabbit or hare can be used.

SERVES 8

140 g (5 oz) pork fat or
  unsmoked bacon
4 rabbit-backs
4 dessertspoons Dijon mustard
1 carrot, sliced
1 large onion, thickly sliced
1 bayleaf, crushed
1 sprig thyme, crushed
salt and pepper
100 g (3½ oz) butter, melted
2 dessertspoons cornflour
500 ml (scant pint) meat stock
200 g (7 oz) fresh cream
1 bunch watercress

1 sharp knife
1 needle for threading the *lardons*
1 flameproof baking dish with
  lid
1 heavy saucepan
1 strainer

The 'râble' is the rabbit's back so you need to chop off the legs and just use the back.

Cut the pork fat or bacon into strips (*lardons*) as thin as matchsticks and about 3 cm (1¼ in) long. Thread the *lardons* through the backs of the rabbits, then coat the backs all over with mustard. Place the sliced carrots in the baking dish, and then add the onion, bayleaf and thyme. Rest the rabbit backs over these, add salt and pepper, pour over the butter and cook, covered, in a moderate oven, 200 °C (400 °F)/Mark 6, for 18–20 minutes. Throughout this cooking time baste very often with the melted butter. When cooked, remove the rabbit backs and keep warm.

Mix the cornflour with a little of the stock and pour this and the rest of the stock into the baking dish. Stir and boil for 5 minutes. Strain through a fine strainer into a small pan, add the cream and boil for 9 minutes. Add salt and pepper if necessary. Cut the backs into four pieces, carefully remove the flesh from the bone in thin slices, and then place these back over the carcasses. Serve with a little of the sauce poured over; the rest served in a sauceboat.

The chef likes to serve *Pommes au Lard* – potatoes with bacon – and fresh green peas with this dish. He adds a bunch of watercress for decoration.

Les Etrennes anglaises.

Milord acceptés ce léger présent. — Oh vite des pommes de terre pour ce bisteck.

A Paris chez Charon, rue St Jean de beauvais, N.° 26   Chez Martinet, Libraire, rue du Coq. N.° 15   et Chez Bance ainé Md d'estampe, rue St Denis, N.° 414

Presented with a small New Year's gift, an Englishman swiftly calls for some potatoes to accompany his ste

LES LÉGUMES

VEGETABLES

Lightly-cooked Vegetables	Les Légumes Légèrement Cuits
Braised Vegetables	Légumes Braisés
Barcelona Spinach	Epinards Barcelona
Brussels Sprouts Limousine (with chestnuts)	Choux de Bruxelles Limousine (avec Marrons)
Chestnut Purée	Purée de Marrons
Brussels Sprouts Cavendish	Choux de Bruxelles Cavendish
Leeks Vinaigrette	Poireaux Vinaigrette
Greek Mushrooms	Champignons à la Grecque
Green Asparagus Tips	Pointes d'Asperges Vertes
Greek Artichokes	Artichauts à la Grecque
Tomatoes Provençale	Tomates Provençale
Aubergine Slices	Rondelles d'Aubergines
Red Cabbage	Chou Rouge
Bacon Potatoes	Pommes de Terre au Lard
Baked Jacket Potatoes	Pommes de Terre en Robe de Chambre
Potato Nuts	Pommes Noisettes
Potatoes Elizabeth	Pommes de Terre Elizabeth
Cream Puff Pastry	Pâte à Choux
Gratin Dauphinois	Gratin Dauphinois
Fresh Noodle Dough	Pâte à Nouilles
Indian Rice	Riz à l'Indienne
Canton Rice	Riz Cantonnais

I have not included in this chapter all the vegetables we serve. And if you find this section rather short it is because, as in an English home – *à l'anglaise* – I like to serve vegetables lightly cooked and not tortured.

It is difficult to serve lightly-cooked vegetables for a large number of guests, even if you have, as we do, help in the kitchen. Vegetables are at their best when lightly boiled, drained and served immediately with a knob of butter and a little freshly-ground pepper. The chef, however, uses this method and he is very successful.

Les Légumes Légèrement Cuits
Lightly-cooked Vegetables

The chef has two pans of boiling salted water – he adds 7 g (1 teaspoon) salt to 1 litre (2 pints) water. He blanches the vegetables first by cooking them for 3 minutes in one pan, strains them and, just before serving, cooks them in the second pan of boiling water. He removes them when they are just cooked; *au croquant* is his phrase and it tastes as it sounds – crisp and not overdone. He then strains them and serves them in a warm dish with knobs of butter.

Légumes Braisés
Braised Vegetables

1 pan boiling salted water
1 buttered oven dish
1 piece fat bacon
a little stock
greaseproof paper

I personally do not like braised vegetables but it is a very French method of cooking some vegetables such as lettuces, leeks, endives, etc. The chef blanches the vegetables as above, then dips them in cold water. He drains and dries them and then places them in a baking dish which has been buttered and has a layer of fat bacon on the bottom. The vegetables are folded if necessary. They are just covered with a little stock, a piece of buttered greaseproof paper is arranged over them and they are cooked in the covered pan in a moderate oven. Cooking time depends on the vegetable. If you wish, the stock can be boiled down and thickened and then poured over the vegetables before serving.

Epinards Barcelona
Barcelona Spinach

This is similar to the filling in the Barcelona Spinach Tart (page 32). It is an original way of serving spinach and is greatly appreciated by guests, who find the mixture intriguing.

SERVES 6–8
1.5 kg (3½ lb) fresh spinach
50 g (1¾ oz) butter for béchamel
25 g (scant oz) butter for tossing
60 g (2 oz) flour, sifted
250 ml (½ pint) hot milk
½ teaspoon nutmeg
60 g (2 oz) pine seeds
100 g (3½ oz) sultanas

1 large pan with lid
1 medium-sized saucepan for béchamel
1 small heavy pan

Cook the spinach for 5 minutes in plenty of lightly-salted boiling water in a covered pan. The chef reckons 7 g (1 teaspoon) salt to 1 litre (2 pints) water. Drain very thoroughly and chop. Cooking time for spinach depends on quality. Make a béchamel (page 121) with butter, flour and milk, then add the nutmeg and spinach. Reheat, allowing spinach to boil for about 2 minutes. Heat the remaining butter in a small pan and toss the sultanas and pine seeds in this. Drain and then add the seeds and sultanas to the spinach. Mix and serve immediately. It is essential to see that the spinach is well drained.

Choux de Bruxelles Limousine (avec Marrons)
Brussels Sprouts Limousine (with Chestnuts)

SERVES 8
400 g (14 oz) chestnuts
250 ml (scant ½ pint) meat stock
1.1 kg (2¼ lb) brussels sprouts, lightly cooked
150 g (5 oz) butter
freshly-ground pepper

1 heavy-bottomed pan

Peel the chestnuts, then put them in boiling water to remove the inner skins. Cook the chestnuts gently in the pan with the stock for 20 minutes. Remove from the heat and drain. Sauté the chestnuts with the brussels sprouts in the butter and serve immediately with a little freshly-ground pepper.

Purée de Marrons
Chestnut Purée

SERVES 8
1.5 kg (3¼ lb) chestnuts
100 g (3½ oz) celery root
   (celeriac), chopped
200 g (7 oz) fresh cream
420 ml (¾ pint) boiling milk
salt and pepper

1 medium-sized pan
1 sieve

Peel the chestnuts and put them in boiling water to remove their inner skins, then cook them with the celery root in lightly-salted water for about 45 minutes. Strain and press through a sieve. Add cream and milk to the purée to obtain the consistency you wish. Check for seasoning and serve in a deep dish. Draw lines across the purée with a fork to decorate.

Choux de Bruxelles Cavendish
Brussels Sprouts Cavendish

I picked up this recipe from the traditional dishes served by Rosa Lewis (the Duchess of Jermyn Street) at the Cavendish Hotel in London. It has now become our favourite way of serving vegetables. It accompanies pies and joints, and French guests find it tasty and original.

SERVES 6–8
1.8 kg (4 lb) brussels sprouts
100 g (3½ oz) butter, melted
500 ml (scant pint) béchamel
   (page 121)
100 g (3½ oz) Cheddar cheese,
   grated
5 slices of bacon, thinly cut and
   grilled

2 large pans lightly-salted water

Note: The cooking times are correct for French sprouts, which are tiny and firm; British sprouts may require less cooking.

Peel the outer leaves off the brussels sprouts, clean and blanch for 4 minutes in lightly-salted water, then drain. Then boil in another pan of lightly salted water (see page 96) for about 20 minutes, taking care that they remain hard. Drain and place in a warmed vegetable dish, pour over the butter and the béchamel, and scatter the grated cheese and the bacon broken up into small pieces over the dish.

You can, if you wish, use more bacon and mix this with the brussels sprouts before adding the béchamel, and scatter still more over the dish with the grated cheese. You can serve immediately or put under the grill to brown.

Poireaux Vinaigrette
Leeks Vinaigrette

This is a good first course for a light lunch. It is a traditional French dish.

SERVES 8
olive oil
vinegar
lemon juice (optional)
2.4 kg (5½ lb) young white leeks
1 dessertspoon parsley, chopped

1 mixing bowl
string
1 large pan
1 deep dish

Make a vinaigrette. The chef's consists of 3 parts olive oil to 1½ parts vinegar or vinegar and lemon juice mixed. It is difficult to give the exact quantity you will need for this recipe, as that depends on the quality of the leeks you use. Make enough to pour over the dish at the end about 400 ml (⅔ pint).

Clean and wash the leeks. Cut them into stumps about 15 cm (6 in) long and tie them in bundles. Boil these for 45 minutes in water with a little salt. Strain the leeks, open the bundles, and cut the leeks in halves lengthwise. Lie them in a dish and pour over the vinaigrette while they are still hot. When cold, arrange the leeks in the serving dish, scatter the chopped parsley over them and serve. You can decorate the dish with lemon slices and you can serve with anchovy fillets, chopped hard-boiled eggs or with capers if you wish.

Champignons à la Grecque
Greek Mushrooms

This is a dish that can be served as an hors d'oeuvre, *or we serve it in the centre of a white bean salad for buffets (page 116). Double the ingredients if you are serving it as a dish by itself for 8. The ingredients below are enough to serve as one of the dishes in an* hors d'oeuvre *or to serve with a bean or rice salad.*

500 g (1 lb) mushrooms
3 onions
200 ml (⅓ pint) olive oil
juice of 2 lemons; grated rind of 1
4 dessertspoons tomato purée

1 heavy pan with lid

Wash, peel and cut the mushrooms if necessary (they are best whole or halved). Slice the onions thinly and fry them in the oil. When golden, add the mushrooms and fry them for a few minutes, then add the lemon juice, the grated rind and the tomato purée. Stir and simmer in covered pan for 30 minutes, stirring from time to time. Allow to cool. Put in refrigerator and serve cold.

Pointes d'Asperges Vertes
Green Asparagus Tips

You can serve these asparagus tips to decorate a dish or as a vegetable.

To decorate a dish with 6 bunches of asparagus:
1.6 kg (3½ lb) small green asparagus

To serve as a vegetable for 6 persons:
2.4 kg (5¼ lb) small green asparagus

1 large pan of lightly-salted boiling water
buttered baking dish
buttered greaseproof paper

Cut off the asparagus stalks to about 6 cm (2½ in) from the beginning of the tips. Make little bundles of these tips and tie them with string. Blanch in lightly-salted boiling water for 4–5 minutes. Plunge into cold water, drain, place in a buttered baking dish, cover with buttered greaseproof paper and cook in a preheated oven, 250 °C (450 °F)/Mark 8, for 4 minutes. Transfer to a warm serving dish and pour over a little melted butter, or use for decorating a dish.

Artichauts à la Grecque
Greek Artichokes

This is an excellent first course and can also be used as part of a mixed hors d'œuvre. *It is best when you can find very small young artichokes.*

SERVES 6–8

12–16 small artichokes
juice of 4 lemons
200 ml (⅓ pint) olive oil
100 g (3½ oz) sliced onions
1 dessertspoon flour
200 ml (⅓ pint) water
100 ml (7 dessertspoons) dry
    white wine
salt and freshly-ground pepper
1 soupspoon fennel or dill,
    chopped
3 carrots, thinly sliced
200 g (7 oz) tiny white onions

1 large bowl of cold water
1 large heavy pan
greaseproof paper

Carefully wash the artichokes and to keep them white drop them into a bowl of water mixed with the juice of 2 lemons. Remove the hairy centre with a stainless steel spoon or the tip of a knife. If the artichokes are small keep them whole; if not, cut in two.

Heat the oil in a heavy pan, add the sliced onions and stir, keeping them white. Add the flour, stir and add the water, wine, salt, pepper, fennel and finally the prepared artichokes, the carrots and whole onions. Pour in the juice of 2 lemons. Cover with buttered greaseproof paper cut to fit the pan and simmer gently for 40–45 minutes. Cool and serve cold with the cooking juices poured over.

If the juices are too light you can reduce them by boiling down, or beat the yolks of 2 eggs with the juice of 2 more lemons and add this to the warm sauce. Stir briskly and allow to cool.

The same method can be used to cook little white onions, mushrooms, fennel and celery, for *hors d'œuvre* or to accompany hams and pâtés. Cook mushrooms for 6–8 minutes; white onions for 35–40 minutes; fennel for 40–50 minutes; and celery hearts for 40–45 minutes.

Tomates Provençale
Tomatoes Provençale

This is a very French dish, usually used for decoration. It is pretty and tastes good – if you do not mind the garlic.

SERVES 8
6 large tomatoes (or 12 small
   ones)
salt
250 g (9 oz) fresh breadcrumbs
1 large clove garlic
freshly-ground pepper
1 soupspoon parsley, chopped
3 soupspoons olive oil

1 kitchen cloth
1 mixing bowl
1 ovenproof dish

Wash the tomatoes, cut them in half and remove seeds. Scatter a little salt over them and lie them upside down on a kitchen cloth for ½ hour so that they dry out a little. Mix the breadcrumbs, garlic, salt, pepper, parsley and the olive oil all together. Spoon this mixture into the tomatoes, then place in a buttered oven dish and cook for 10–15 minutes in a very hot oven, 220 °C (425 °F)/Mark 7.

Serve separately in a vegetable dish or round a joint. Before bringing the tomatoes to the table, scatter a little chopped parsley over them.

Rondelles d'Aubergines
Aubergine Slices

The chef often decorates his dishes with these aubergines, which look as if they have stripes down their sides. He also serves them as a vegetable in a deep vegetable dish.

SERVES 8
8 aubergines, weighing about
   250 g (½ lb) each
200 g (7 oz) butter
1 dessertspoon olive oil
salt and pepper
1 dessertspoon parsley, chopped

1 sharp knife
1 lemon dresser
1 heavy-bottomed frying or
   sauté pan
1 baking dish

Wash the aubergines and use a pointed knife or preferably a lemon dresser to carve out grooves down the sides of the aubergines, lifting out the skin. Cut the aubergines into round slices about 2.5 cm (1 in) thick and make criss-cross marks in their flesh on both sides with the point of a knife. Heat the butter and oil in a heavy-bottomed pan and sauté the aubergine slices until they are golden. Add the salt and pepper. Remove the slices and place them in a baking dish (side by side, not one on top of the other) and bake in a moderate oven, 200 °C (400 °F)/Mark 6, for 10 minutes. Turn out into a serving dish or arrange round a meat dish, and decorate with chopped parsley.

Chou Rouge
Red Cabbage

We serve red cabbage with game pie. There are various ways of cooking the cabbage, and you can adapt our recipe.

SERVES 6

4 onions, sliced
5 dessertspoons fat or dripping
2 dessertspoons sugar
1.5 kg (3½ lb) red cabbage, shredded
4 dessertspoons vinegar
250 ml (scant ½ pint) white wine
250 ml (scant ½ pint) stock or water
5 whole peppercorns (or 1 dessertspoon caraway seeds)
salt
2 apples, peeled, cored and sliced

1 heavy-bottomed pan with lid

Fry the onions in the fat, add the sugar, stir and add the shredded cabbage. Toss and add the vinegar and cook for a few minutes. Then add the wine, stock, and the peppercorns or caraway seeds. Cover and cook gently for 1½ hours. Halfway through cooking time test for salt and add the apples. Serve hot or cold.

Note: You can, if you wish, add 2 dessertspoons of sultanas or currants.

Pommes de Terre au Lard
Bacon Potatoes

SERVES 8

1.5 kg (3½ lb) potatoes
150 g (5 oz) lean bacon
100 g (3½ oz) butter
20 tiny onions, peeled
1 generous soupspoon flour
150 g (5 oz) tomato *fondue* (page 126)
1 *bouquet garni* (parsley, rosemary, celery, bay)
1 litre (2 pints) stock
chopped parsley to garnish

1 heavy pan with lid

Choose firm potatoes for this dish, and peel them. The chef peels them by cutting the peel round and round like a snake. That leaves him with a potato looking rather like a large olive. Cut the bacon in strips, blanch it for 5 minutes and drain. Heat the butter in the heavy pan and toss the bacon, onions and the flour in this until well browned. Add the *fondue* of tomato, the *bouquet garni*, the stock and the potatoes. Mix, and place in a preheated moderate oven, 200 °C (400 °F)/Mark 6, for about 20 minutes. Serve in a vegetable dish with chopped parsley scattered over it.

Pommes de Terre en Robe de Chambre
Baked Jacket Potatoes

There are many ways of doing baked potatoes. One of my favourite ways is to wash them, and while they are still wet, coat them with thick salt, then put them in the oven. But the chef has a very good recipe (he adds to my method) which he uses for buffets or to serve with Scottish roast beef.

SERVES 8
16 potatoes, each weighing about
   80 g (2½ oz)
100 g (3½ oz) butter
1 soupspoon parsley, chopped
pinch grated nutmeg
salt and pepper
50 g (1¾ oz) Gruyère cheese,
   grated

1 baking tray
1 mixing bowl

Wash the potatoes and cut the skins all the way round so that each potato has a 'lid'. Thickly coat them with salt and cook in a moderate oven, 200 °C (400 °F)/Mark 6, for 45–50 minutes. Take off the lids (and keep them warm if you wish) and empty the potatoes without damaging the skins. Mix the potato with the butter, parsley, nutmeg, salt and freshly-ground pepper. (The chef likes to use a fork here so as to leave little pieces of potato whole.) Fill the potato skins with this mixture, cover with the grated Gruyère and place in the oven for a further 15 minutes. Replace the lids and serve in a deep dish on a folded napkin.

Pommes Noisettes
Potato Nuts

These are rounds cut out of potatoes with a special cutter. In France it is called a pommes noisette *spoon, in England it is called a potato-ball cutter. It can be used to cut carrots, too. A member of our Embassy's little son was so impressed by these potatoes and carrots that he asked his father – quite seriously – if when he became Ambassador he would be able to grow vegetables that came out all the same size.*

SERVES 8
1.6 kg (3¼ lb) potato balls cut out
   of potatoes
150 g (5 oz) butter
salt

1 large pan
1 heavy pan with lid

Blanch the potato balls for 2–3 minutes in lightly-salted boiling water, then cook gently in a heavy pan with the butter. Turn and shake the balls often, and remove them when they are well browned. Add salt to taste while they are cooking.

Pommes de Terre Elizabeth
Potatoes Elizabeth

This is a soufflé potato with spinach inside it. It is light and unexpected. The spinach is inserted at the last minute so that it does not become overcooked.

SERVES 8

500 g (1 lb) potatoes, peeled
100 g (3½ oz) butter
yolks of 4 eggs
200 g (7 oz) choux pastry (see below)
salt and pepper
nutmeg
oil for frying
300 g (10 oz) spinach
200 ml (⅓ pint) béchamel (page 121)

1 large pan
1 sieve
1 medium-sized heavy saucepan
1 deep frying pan

Cook the potatoes in lightly-salted water for 20 minutes. Drain and leave to dry out for about 4 minutes in a heated oven with the door open. Put the potatoes through a sieve and then into a heavy saucepan with the butter. Stir to allow any remaining water to evaporate. Cool, then add the egg yolks, choux pastry, salt, pepper and nutmeg. Take a soup spoon, fill it with some potato mixture and drop it in a deep frying pan filled with vegetable oil. The temperature of the oil should be 150 °C (300 °F) and the frying time should be about 6 minutes. You should try to do 10 spoonfuls at a time. Remove and drain the potato balls when they are golden, cut a hole in them with the point of a kitchen knife and fill each one with the previously washed, cooked and chopped spinach which has been mixed with a little béchamel sauce.

Serve as a decoration round meat dishes or separately in a warmed dish.

Pâte à Choux
Cream Puff Pastry

¼ litre (½ pint) water
75 g (2½ oz) butter
½ teaspoon salt
1 teaspoon sugar (for sweet choux)
pinch grated nutmeg
100 g (generous) (4 oz) flour
4 eggs

1 heavy-bottomed pan
1 mixer or whisk
1 wooden spoon
1 mixing bowl

Heat the butter, salt, sugar (if used) and nutmeg in the water and bring to the boil. Remove from heat and add the sifted flour all at once. Beat rapidly and return to the fire, lowering the heat. Continue beating the mixture until it dries out and leaves the sides of the pan. Remove and incorporate the eggs, one at a time, beating briskly. (This is done more easily in a mixer.) Beat well after the last egg has been added. (Left-over mixture can be wrapped in foil and frozen – it keeps well.) This makes about 500 g (1 lb) of pastry.

Gratin Dauphinois

A traditional French dish to serve eight.

1.6 kg (3½ lb) potatoes
150 g (5 oz) Gruyère or Cheddar
  cheese, grated
750 ml (1¼ pints) fresh cream
2 eggs
1 clove garlic, crushed
salt and pepper
chopped parsley to garnish

1 40-cm (16-in) oval gratin dish

Cut the potatoes in thin round slices. Put a layer of potatoes in the greased oven dish, followed by one layer of cheese. Continue in alternate layers until the dish is full, ending with a layer of cheese. Mix the cream with the eggs, garlic, salt and pepper and pour over the dish so that the potatoes are completely covered. Place in a preheated moderate oven, 200 °C (400 °F)/Mark 6, for 50–60 minutes. Scatter a little chopped parsley over the top before serving.

Pâte à Nouilles
Fresh Noodle Dough

SERVES 8–9
600 g (1 lb 5 oz) flour, sifted
4 eggs
2 dessertspoons vegetable oil
salt
100 g (3½ oz) butter
100 g (3½ oz) fresh cream
  (optional)

1 mixing bowl
1 pastry board
4 clean kitchen cloths
1 large pan

Mix together the flour, eggs, oil, 2 dessertspoons water and a pinch of salt, and knead the ingredients into a firm dough on a floured pastry board. Allow to stand for 2 hours, covered with a clean cloth in a cool place. Roll out very, very thinly, scatter a little flour over the pastry and cut it into strips about 1 cm (½ in) wide. Cut these again, so that each strip is about 5 cm (2 in) long. Lie the strips on cloths to dry for about 1 hour and then cook in boiling salted water for 6 minutes. Drain, add the butter and, if you wish, fresh cream. Serve immediately.

Vary the recipe by making green noodles (*nouilles vertes*). It is difficult to predict the quantity of spinach for a *purée*; it depends on the quality of the spinach and how much of the stalks you have to remove. For this recipe you need 300 g (10 oz) cooked spinach which has been pressed through a sieve. That is the way the chef does it. You can put it in a liquidizer and then drain it well, but it will take some time to remove all the liquid. It's best to leave the spinach overnight as it is essential that the spinach *purée* is drained of all water.

Make green noodles according to the recipe above, but allow the rolled out pasta to dry for 15–20 minutes before cutting. The dough will, of course, be softer than before.

Riz à l'Indienne
Indian Rice

SERVES 8
500 g (1 lb 2 oz) rice
5 litres (8½ pints) water
salt

1 large pan
1 strainer
1 large baking tin
1 clean kitchen cloth

Wash the rice and cook it in a pan of boiling salted water for about 16 minutes from the moment that the water boils. Allow 10 g (1½ teaspoons) salt per litre (2 pints) water. Drain the rice, wash in tepid water, drain again, spread it on a clean kitchen cloth on a large baking tin and leave it to dry out in a very cool oven. At the Embassy we lie it in a preheated, very slow oven with the door open, for about 20 minutes.

Riz Cantonnais
Canton Rice

SERVES 8
100 g (3½ oz) ham
100 g (3½ oz) young peas
2 eggs
salt and pepper
1 small onion, chopped
150 g (5 oz) butter
300 g (10 oz) rice
600 ml (1 pint) water

1 mixing bowl
1 saucepan
1 small heavy pan with lid for
  eggs
1 medium-sized heavy pan with
  lid

This is a delicious way of serving rice. We serve it as an accompaniment to duck or veal dishes. It can also be served as an entrée or first course with poached eggs around it, or as a ring of rice surrounding œufs mollets (page 172).

Cut the ham into strips about 2.5 cm (1 in) long. Cook the peas in boiling salted water for 5 minutes. Break the eggs into a bowl and beat them, then add salt and pepper. Pour the egg mixture into a small pan coated with a teaspoon of vegetable oil, cover, and leave the pan on the side of the fire until the eggs are cooked. Remove this 'flat omelette' and cut it into strips like the ham.

Toss the onion in the heavy, medium-sized pan with the butter and add the rice, and some salt and pepper. Stir and add the water. Cover, bring to the boil and then cook gently for about 18 minutes. When the rice is cooked, add the ham, eggs and peas. Mix gently with a fork, cover, and stand the pan on the side of the fire until you wish to serve.

Le Thé Anglais.

Tea the English way

SALADES

SALADS

Mixed Green Salad	Salade Verte Composée
Frizzy Bacon Salad	Salade Frisée au Lard
Watercress and Radish Salad	Salade de Cresson et de Radis
Waldorf Salad	Salade Waldorf
Finocchio or Florence Fennel Salad	Salade de Fenouil
Niçoise Salad	Salade Niçoise
Cauliflower Salad	Salade de Chou-Fleur
Artichoke and Fennel (Finocchio) Salad	Salade d'Artichauts au Fenouil
Mayonnaise Gâteau	Gâteau Mayonnaise
Broad Bean and Mint Salad	Salade de Fèves à la Menthe
White Bean Salad	Salade de Haricots Blancs
Spanish Rice Salad	Salade de Riz à L'Espagnole

Salade Verte Composée
Mixed Green Salad

There is nothing better than a really good green salad, and nothing worse than a tired one. Funnily enough, the French expression for tossing a salad is *fatiguer la salade* – which does mean to tire it. But in fact all it really means is to toss it well just before serving. And a good French lettuce salad with the right amount of dressing and a little chopped parsley is a real delight.

You can choose either a plain lettuce or a plain chicory salad or a lettuce and cucumber salad, a mixture of endives and watercress, etc. But the important touch in all salads is the dressing. Some cooks mix the dressing over the salad, pouring in the vinegar and oil without measuring. Here are the basic quantities for a good dressing. And remember that the salad *must* be dry after washing – dry out all the ingredients on a cloth or a piece of kitchen paper, and toss in the following mixture:

2 dessertspoons vinegar or lemon juice
6–8 dessertspoons olive oil (you can mix olive and vegetable oil if you wish)
salt and freshly-ground pepper to taste
any mixture of chopped parsley, mint, tarragon, dill, rosemary, capers, etc. and a little mustard

Note: It is important to mix the salt, pepper, herbs and mustard with the vinegar first, and then add the oil.

Salade Frisée au Lard
Frizzy Bacon Salad

This is a salad which makes a delicious first course. It should be tossed at the last moment and therefore at the Embassy we only serve it for small lunches and dinners.

SERVES 8
2 fresh chicory
4 hard-boiled eggs, sliced
2 dessertspoons vinegar or lemon juice
salt and freshly-ground pepper
1 dessertspoon ready-made Colman's mustard
6–8 dessertspoons olive oil and vegetable oil mixed, or olive oil only
2 dessertspoons chopped parsley
4 thick slices of bacon, diced

1 large salad bowl
1 mixing bowl
1 heavy-bottomed pan

Wash the chicory and pick out the freshest leaves. Dry them and arrange them in a large salad bowl. Add the hard-boiled eggs. In a separate bowl, mix the lemon juice or vinegar, salt, pepper, mustard and oil. Pour this over the salad, and scatter the chopped parsley. Do not toss. Heat the bacon in a heavy-bottomed pan and pour over the salad. Toss and serve immediately.

Salade de Cresson et de Radis
Watercress and Radish Salad

The interesting thing about this salad is the dressing, but it is essential to toss the salad at the last minute so that the watercress remains fresh.

SERVES 8
2–3 bunches watercress
1–2 bunches radishes
60 g (2 oz) stem ginger, cut in very thin slices (*julienne*)
150 ml (¼ pint) vegetable oil
2 dessertspoons olive oil
juice of 1 large lemon
salt and pepper

1 salad bowl
1 bowl to mix dressing

Wash and trim the watercress. I like to leave it in largish sprigs. Slice the radishes very thinly and mix with the watercress in a salad bowl. Mix the ginger into the oils (use only olive oil if you prefer) and lemon juice, add salt and pepper, beat and pour over the salad. Toss just before serving.

Salade Waldorf
Waldorf Salad

This is a traditional American salad. We like to serve it at buffets.

SERVES 8

400 g (14 oz) celery, diced
100 g (3½ oz) walnuts
400 g (14 oz) apples, diced
juice of 1 lemon
1 dessertspoon olive oil
300 g (10½ oz) mayonnaise (page 124)
salt and pepper

2 saucepans
1 mixing bowl

Blanch the celery for 4 minutes in lightly-salted water, then drain and dry. Blanch and skin the walnuts if you wish (the chef does). Mix together all the celery, walnuts and apples and add the lemon juice and olive oil. Leave to macerate for 1 hour, tossing from time to time. Before serving mix with the mayonnaise, check taste for salt and pepper and scatter a little chopped parsley over it if you wish. The salad should be served chilled.

A lighter salad can be made by cutting the celery into *julienne* strips, slicing the apple very thinly, adding the walnuts and tossing the salad in a dressing of 150 ml (¼ pint) vegetable oil, the juice of 1 lemon, and salt and pepper to taste.

Note: In France we use *reinette* apples.

Salade de Fenouil
Finocchio or Florence Fennel Salad

SERVES 8

1.5 kg (3½ lb) of the bulbous base of *Finocchio* or fennel
100 g (3½ oz) carrots, thinly sliced
1 dessertspoon parsley, chopped
1 dessertspoon fennel leaves, chopped
200 ml (⅓ pint) vegetable oil
100 ml (⅕ pint) olive oil
4 dessertspoons lemon juice
salt and pepper
1 lemon for decoration, sliced and serrated

1 large pan
1 large mixing bowl
1 small mixing bowl for dressing

Note: In French the fennel bases are called *pieds de fenouil.*

Trim the Finocchio, wash it and cook it in a pan of lightly-salted boiling water for 20 minutes. Drain. Blanch the carrot *julienne* for 2 minutes and drain. Quarter the fennel bases (if they are large cut them into 8 or 12 slices) and arrange the fennel in a large mixing bowl with the carrot strips. In a separate bowl, mix half the parsley and the fennel leaves with the oils, lemon juice, salt and pepper. Pour this over the fennel and carrot mixture and toss well. Leave to macerate for about 1 hour, tossing from time to time. Serve in a deep dish with the rest of the parsley and fennel leaves scattered over it and, if you wish, decorate the dish with lemon slices.

Salade Niçoise
Niçoise Salad

There are many variations of this salad and we like to vary it according to whether it is to be a light entrée or a more substantial part of a cold buffet. It is a traditional French salad and should be tossed and served freshly, not prepared and left in the refrigerator. The ingredients can of course be prepared in advance but the mixing must be left to the end.

SERVES 8

500 g (1 lb) French beans
500 g (1 lb) firm potatoes
500 g (1 lb) firm salad tomatoes
salt
50 g (1¾ oz) capers
100 g (3½ oz) small black olives
5 dessertspoons olive oil
2 dessertspoons vinegar (or vinegar and lemon juice mixed)
1 teaspoon basil or tarragon, chopped (optional)
freshly-ground black pepper
2 hard-boiled eggs, sliced
16 anchovy fillets

2 saucepans
1 large mixing bowl
1 small mixing bowl for dressing

Lightly cook the beans so that they remain firm. Cook the potatoes in their skins, then peel and slice. Peel the tomatoes by dropping them into boiling water for a few seconds. Slice them and remove seeds. Scatter a little salt over them, then drain. Remove stones from olives. Put the beans, potatoes, tomatoes, capers and olives into a large mixing bowl. Mix the oil, vinegar, basil, salt and freshly-ground pepper and pour over the salad. Toss and mix well. Decorate with hard-boiled eggs and anchovy fillets and serve.

You can, if you like, add any of the following:

3 sweet peppers (remove seeds and cut into strips)
3 green peppers (remove seeds and cut into strips)
300 g (10 oz) fresh peas, lightly cooked
300 g (10 oz) mushrooms, peeled, sliced and tossed in lemon juice
1 dessertspoon chopped onion or a bunch of fresh young onions, peeled and left whole
tunny fish divided into large pieces

You can also, if you wish, pound the anchovy fillets with the basil, a clove of garlic, the yolk of 1 egg and the olives. Beat this into the dressing, toss the salad and serve.

Salade de Chou-Fleur
Cauliflower Salad

Raw cauliflower makes a good crunchy salad. You can vary this one depending on your favourite ingredients and taste.

SERVES 6
1 fresh white cauliflower
250 g (½ lb) mushrooms
juice of ½ lemon
2–3 small young onions
1 bunch radishes
1 bunch watercress
250 g (½ lb) ham, diced

1 large bowl

For the dressing:
2 dessertspoons vinegar
juice of ½ lemon
1 dessertspoon double cream or
    yoghourt
2 teaspoons caper, chopped
125 g (4½ oz) walnuts, chopped
salt and freshly-ground pepper
6–8 dessertspoons olive oil

1 small bowl

Wash the cauliflower and cut it into small bunches. Slice the mushrooms and squeeze half the lemon juice over them. Slice the young onions, and shape the radishes into 'flowers', cutting the petals with a sharp knife and making small cuts all round the radishes. Leave them in ice-cold water to open. Wash and pick the watercress.

Place the cauliflower, mushrooms, onions, watercress and ham in a mixing bowl and toss them all in the dressing. Mix the dressing in a separate bowl and pour over salad just before serving. Decorate with the radish 'flowers'.

Note: Boiled shrimps or bacon crisply fried and diced can be substituted for the ham, and you can vary the dressing by adding 3 dessertspoons of pounded Roquefort cheese.

Salade d'Artichauts au Fenouil
Artichoke and Fennel Salad

SERVES 8
15 artichoke hearts
1 fennel base (the bulbous part)
1 medium-sized onion, chopped
1 *bouquet garni* (thyme, parsley, bayleaf)
7 dessertspoons olive oil
juice of 1 lemon
salt and pepper
2 generous dessertspoons parsley, chopped

1 heavy pan with lid
1 mixing bowl for salad
1 mixing bowl for dressing

If you are using whole artichokes, prepare the hearts as in the recipe on page 24. Cut the artichoke hearts into 6 or 8 pieces. Thinly slice the fennel base. Put the artichokes, fennel and onion into a heavy pan or *cocotte*. Add the *bouquet garni* and 500 ml (1 pint) water. Cook, covered, for 30 minutes. Drain and leave to cool. Toss the salad in an oil and lemon dressing and serve in a deep dish with chopped parsley scattered over it. Decorate, if you wish, with lemon slices. Serve cold.

Gâteau Mayonnaise
Mayonnaise Gâteau

I first had this in Chile and have served it in all our posts since. An original way of serving a mixed salad, it is a pretty first course if you want something light and fresh, and also looks decorative on a buffet.

SERVES 6–8
4 hard-boiled eggs
250 ml (scant ½ pint) mayonnaise (page 124)
1 kg (2 lb) firm tomatoes
750 g (1½ lb) lightly cooked french beans

1 22.5-cm (9-in) cake tin with removable base and rim
1 plate

Place one layer of sliced hard-boiled eggs on the bottom of the tin. Carefully spread a little mayonnaise on the eggs so that these will stick to the next layer only, not to the tin. Then add a layer of sliced tomatoes. Carefully mix the remaining slices of tomato and the beans with mayonnaise and continue placing alternate layers of beans, tomatoes and eggs until the tin is full. Press down well and cover with a plate. Place in a cold part of the refrigerator for 4 hours at least, or in the freezer for 2 hours. When you are ready to serve the cake, upturn it on a round dish and remove the rim and base of the tin. For formal occasions you can serve this dish with a frill of salami slices or a ring of shrimps.

Note: The chef prefers to line his cake tin with greaseproof paper, which he wets with cold water. He finds it easier and neater to unmould.

Salade de Fèves à la Menthe
Broad Bean and Mint Salad

This makes a fresh and easy salad and a change from mixed green salads.

SERVES 8

1.6 kg (3½ lb) broad beans, shelled and skinned
1 sprig mint
150 ml (¼ pint) vegetable oil
5 dessertspoons olive oil
2 dessertspoons lemon juice
1 dessertspoon fresh mint, chopped
salt and pepper

1 large pan
1 strainer
1 large mixing bowl

Cook the beans in a large pan of lightly salted water with a sprig of mint in it for 4–5 minutes. Remove, drain and pour over some cold water to cool. Drain the beans well and when they are still lukewarm place them in a bowl and toss in the oil, lemon juice, chopped mint, salt and pepper. Toss from time to time until cold. Serve cold with a little chopped mint scattered over the dish.

Salade de Haricots Blancs
White Bean Salad

SERVES 8

500 g (1 lb) best quality dried white beans
2 onions, quartered
2 celery stalks

For the dressing:
7 dessertspoons lemon juice
1 teaspoon salt
freshly-ground pepper
3 dessertspoons parsley, chopped
3 dessertspoons capers
1½ dessertspoons thyme or rosemary, chopped
200 ml (7 oz) olive oil

1 large pan
1 large mixing bowl
1 small mixing bowl for dressing

Leave the beans to soak overnight covered in warm water. The next day, bring them to the boil, and add the onions and celery stalks. Cook until tender, without salt. Drain and remove onions and celery. Cooking time varies from 1½–2 hours depending on the quality of the beans. Strain. Beat together the remaining ingredients to make a dressing, and pour this over the beans while they are still hot. Toss carefully and allow to cool. Serve cold with Greek mushrooms (page 100) piled up on the centre.

Salade de Riz à L'Espagnole
Spanish Rice Salad

This is a salad we like to serve for buffets. It is an excellent accompaniment for cold meat or fish dishes. You can vary it and use it as an entrée by mixing in a medium-sized tin of tunny fish and decorating the dish with lightly cooked shrimps tossed in the dressing.

Cook the rice in a large pan of lightly-salted water for 16 minutes. Allow 7 g (1 teaspoon) salt to 1 litre (2 pints) water. Drain the rice and add the onions, olives, red pepper, tomatoes, garlic and parsley. Mix the remaining ingredients to make the dressing, and toss the salad in the dressing while the rice is still warm. Leave salad to cool and serve cold in a deep bowl decorated with slices of lemon and a little chopped parsley scattered over the dish.

SERVES 8

500 g (1 lb) rice
50 g (1¾ oz) white onions, chopped
50 g (1¾ oz) large green olives, stones removed
50 g (1¾ oz) black olives, stones removed
1 large red pepper, cut into strips
3 tomatoes, skinned, sliced and pips removed
1 small clove garlic, crushed and chopped
1 dessertspoon parsley, chopped

For the dressing:
200 ml (⅓ pint) olive oil
150 ml (¼ pint) vegetable oil
100 ml (⅕ pint) lemon juice
grated rind of 1 lemon
salt and pepper

1 large pan
1 large mixing bowl
1 small bowl for dressing

MILORD POUF, CHEZ COUPON TAILLEUR

Déposé à la Direction de la Librairie

The English 'Milord Pouf' being fitted at the tailors

LES SAUCES

SAUCES

The Chef's Sauce for Boiled and Braised Meat	Sauce du Chef pour Viandes Bouillies
The Chef's Sauce for Grilled Meat	Sauce du Chef pour Viandes Grillées
Béchamel Sauce	Sauce Béchamel
Choron Sauce	Sauce Choron
Cumberland Sauce	Sauce Cumberland
Devil Sauce	Sauce Diable
Hollandaise Sauce	Sauce Hollandaise
Madeira Sauce	Sauce Madère
Mayonnaise	Mayonnaise
Mint Sauce	Sauce à la Menthe
Apple and Mint Jelly	Gelée de Pommes à la Menthe
Nantua Sauce	Sauce Nantua
Portuguese Tomato Fondue	Fondue de Tomate Portugaise
Horseradish Sauce	Sauce Raifort
Rémoulade Sauce	Sauce Rémoulade
Smitane Sauce	Sauce Smitane
Tartar Sauce	Sauce Tartare
Green Sauce	Sauce Verte
Caramel Sauce	Sauce Caramel
Chocolate Sauce	Sauce au Chocolat
Brandy Butter	Beurre au Cognac
Raspberry Sauce	Sauce Framboise
Fruit Sauce	Sauce aux Fruits
Ginger Sauce	Sauce Gingembre

Sauce du Chef pour Viandes Bouillies
The Chef's Sauce for Boiled and Braised Meat

4 ripe tomatoes
3 hard-boiled eggs
4 anchovy fillets
1 small clove garlic
2 teaspoons Colman's powdered
    mustard
500 ml (scant pint) vegetable oil
juice of 1 lemon
2 teaspoons Worcestershire sauce
1 dessertspoon parsley, chopped
2 teaspoons basil, chopped

1 heavy saucepan
1 liquidizer

Skin the tomatoes by dropping them into boiling water for a few seconds, and remove the pips. Put the tomatoes in a liquidizer with the hard-boiled eggs, anchovy, garlic, and mustard. Switch on the liquidizer and add the oil gradually. Finally add the lemon juice, Worcestershire sauce, parsley and basil.

Sauce du Chef pour Viandes Grillées
The Chef's Sauce for Grilled Meat

SERVES 6–8
200 g (7 oz) onion, chopped
1 small clove garlic
100 ml ($\frac{1}{5}$ pint) vegetable oil
200 ml ($\frac{1}{3}$ pint) water
200 ml ($\frac{1}{3}$ pint) tomato ketchup
1 dessertspoon Worcestershire
    sauce
2 dessertspoons vinegar
salt, pepper and paprika
1 teaspoon Colman's powdered
    mustard
$\frac{1}{2}$ teaspoon cayenne pepper
1 bayleaf

1 heavy saucepan

Toss the onion and garlic lightly in the oil, mix in the rest of the ingredients and cook gently for 25 minutes. Remove bayleaf and serve.

Sauce Béchamel
Béchamel Sauce

30 g (1 oz) butter
30 g (1 oz) flour
500 ml (scant pint) hot milk
salt and pepper

1 heavy pan
1 whisk

Gently heat the butter in a heavy pan, add the flour, and stir. Pour in the previously heated milk all at once and beat with a wire whisk until the mixture is just on the boil. (If you are adding cheese, cream or eggs, as indicated in several of the recipes, remove pan from the heat to do so.) This makes a generous 500 ml (scant pint) sauce.

Note: The chef removes the béchamel from the fire when it has boiled, stirs it well and then puts the pan back on the stove to simmer for 10–15 minutes.

Sauce Choron
Choron Sauce

20 ml (2 dessertspoons) vinegar
1 shallot, chopped
1 teaspoon tarragon, chopped
2 peppercorns, crushed
yolks of 3 eggs
200 g (7 oz) butter, melted
1 dessertspoon concentrated
   tomato paste
salt

1 medium-sized saucepan to fit
   inside a larger pan for
   bain-marie
1 whisk

Heat the vinegar, shallot, tarragon and peppercorns until the sauce has reduced its volume by a quarter, then add 2 dessertspoons cold water. Remove from fire and add the egg yolks. Beat the mixture with a whisk in a double boiler over boiling water. Gradually add the butter and finally the tomato paste and salt to taste. This makes a generous 500 ml (scant pint) sauce.

Sauce Cumberland
Cumberland Sauce

We serve this sauce with all cold meats and game, on buffets and with pâtés.

20 g (⅔ oz) shallots
30 g (1 oz) orange peel
30 g (1 oz) lemon peel
120 g (4 oz) redcurrant jelly
1 teaspoon Colman's English mustard
pinch cayenne pepper
pinch powdered ginger
100 ml (⅕ pint) port
juice of ½ orange

2 saucepans
1 mixing bowl

Chop and blanch the shallots. Blanch the orange and lemon peel – use only the outer peel (pith removed), cut into narrow strips. Mix all the ingredients and allow to macerate for a day before serving. This makes 250 ml (scant ½ pint) of sauce.

Sauce Diable
Devil Sauce

This is a sauce the chef uses to accompany grilled veal and chicken and generally white meat.

2 good-sized shallots, chopped
50 g (1¾ oz) butter
300 ml (½ pint) dry white wine
pepper
300 ml (½ pint) strong meat stock
salt
1 teaspoon Colman's powdered mustard
10 drops Worcestershire sauce

1 small heavy pan

Fry the shallots in the butter, add the white wine and a pinch of pepper. Boil until the sauce has reduced its volume by half. Add the stock, salt and mustard and Worcestershire sauce. This makes 400 ml (⅔ pint) sauce.

Sauce Hollandaise
Hollandaise Sauce

SERVES 6
3 egg yolks
250 g (½ lb) melted tepid butter
salt and pepper
juice of ½ lemon

1 heavy saucepan
1 large pan for *bain-marie*

Put the egg yolks and 4 dessertspoons water in a heavy pan and beat gently for 1–2 minutes. Then stand the saucepan in another pan containing simmering water and continue to beat. Gradually incorporate the tepid butter, beating all the time, and finally, when the sauce has thickened, remove pan and add salt, pepper and lemon juice.

The sauce is best served immediately but if you have to keep it for about an hour, keep in a pan of warm water.

A Hollandaise is a delicate and difficult sauce to make and it does curdle unless beating and heating is gradual. If the cooking process is too rapid, you can stop it by quickly removing the pan from the heat and plunging it into cold water, or by adding a piece of chilled butter.

Sauce Madère
Madeira Sauce

80 g (2¾ oz) butter
60 g (2 oz) flour, sifted
25 g (1 oz) carrots, diced
10 g (2 teaspoons) chopped onion
10 g (2 teaspoons) bacon, diced
2½ dessertspoons white wine
1 small branch or 1 teaspoon thyme
1 litre (2 pints) meat stock (page 173)
50 g (1¾ oz) tomato purée
salt and pepper
100 ml (⅕ pint) Madeira

1 small heavy saucepan
1 medium-sized heavy saucepan
1 fine strainer

In a small heavy pan make a *roux* – that is to say gently heat 50 g (1¾ oz) butter and the flour, stir, and cook until it has taken on a brown colour.

In another pan toss the carrot, onion and bacon with the remaining butter. When well tossed, add the wine and stir, scraping the bottom of the saucepan so as to incorporate all the juices. Then add the *roux*, the thyme and the hot meat stock. Cook gently for 20 minutes, strain through a fine strainer, add the tomato purée and salt and pepper and simmer very gently, skimming quite often until the sauce has reduced its volume by half. Put through the strainer again. Add the Madeira and check the flavour for salt and pepper, adding more if necessary.

Mayonnaise

yolks of 3 eggs
1 teaspoon Colman's mustard
salt and pepper
500 ml (scant pint) oil

1 mixing bowl
1 whisk

Drop the egg yolks into a mixing bowl, add the mustard, salt and pepper and stir. (The chef does this with a small egg whisk.) Add the oil gradually, then check seasoning. (We use vegetable oil, but you can, of course, use olive oil.) If the mayonnaise is too thick, add a little tepid water. The chef insists that the success of a mayonnaise depends on the yolks, oil and kitchen all being at the same temperature.

If you want your mayonnaise to be white, add a dessert-spoon of vinegar or lemon juice. And to prevent it from separating the chef adds a tablespoon of boiling water at the end of the thickening process.

This makes 600 ml (generous pint) of mayonnaise.

Sauce à la Menthe
Mint Sauce

3 dessertspoons castor sugar
5 dessertspoons mint, chopped
150 ml ($\frac{1}{4}$ pint) vinegar

1 small mixing bowl

Mint sauce is the traditional sauce that accompanies lamb and mutton in Britain. We have served it in Paris and I must admit that quite a number of my guests looked in horror at this sweet-sour sauce. But those who liked it were enthusiastic, so here is the recipe we use.

Mix the sugar and mint and chop together very finely. Place in sauceboat, add 3 dessertspoons boiling water, and then the vinegar. Allow to cool. This makes about 200 ml ($\frac{1}{3}$ pint) sauce.

Gelée de Pommes à la Menthe
Apple and Mint Jelly

1 kg (2 lb) cooking apples
2 sprigs mint
2 litres (3½ pints) water
2 kg (4½ lb) sugar
juice of 3 lemons

2 heavy-bottomed pans
1 piece of muslin or cloth
1 strainer
warmed clean jam jars

We like to serve this jelly with lamb as a change from the traditional mint sauce. It is made in advance and used when required.

Wash, quarter and core the apples, but do not peel. Put them in a pan with the sprigs of mint and water to cover. Simmer gently for 45 minutes. When the apples are cooked, pour into a strainer lined with a piece of muslin or a cloth and allow to decant into a clean bowl. Put the juice in a clean pan with the sugar and lemon juice (the equivalent quantities of sugar to juice are: 500 g (1 lb 2 oz) sugar to 500 ml (scant pint) apple juice). Cook rapidly, removing scum. Test as for jam – i.e. when a drop tested on a cold plate sets, the jelly is ready. Remove from the fire, allow to stand for 10 minutes and then pour into clean, warmed jam jars. You can seal the jars the following day with a piece of greaseproof paper dipped in glycerine, or use any favourite method of sealing jam.

You can, if you wish, add 2 dessertspoons of very finely chopped mint at the end of the boiling. You can also crush some mint in the sugar you use for the jelly. This recipe makes about 1.5 litres (2½ pints) jelly.

Sauce Nantua
Nantua Sauce

15 prawns
1 litre (2 pints) vegetable stock
  (page 174)
100 g (3½ oz) butter
200 ml (⅓ pint) fresh cream
500 ml (scant pint) béchamel
  sauce (page 121)
salt and white pepper
pinch cayenne pepper

1 mortar
1 medium-sized pan to fit into
  double boiler for *bain-marie*
1 fine-meshed sieve

Wash the prawns and, if not cleaned, remove their intestinal sacs. This is a delicate operation and if you have to do it yourself, it is best to use a pointed knife and make a slit on the under side of the tail, then pull the sac gently so that it does not break and give the prawns a bitter taste. Cook the prawns for 10 minutes in the stock.

Remove and shell the prawn tails, then cut them lengthwise into two. Pound all the prawn shells in a mortar with the butter. (You can put the shells through a mincer with large holes, but pounding is better.) Put the debris in a pan in a double boiler or *bain-marie*. Stir as the mixture heats to dissolve the butter. Cover with water, stir, heat up for 15 minutes. Strain through a fine sieve, pressing so that the water separates from the butter. Cool, to collect the congealed butter mixture.

Add the fresh cream to the béchamel and heat gently until it has lost approximately a quarter of its volume. Then add the prawn butter, the salt, white pepper, cayenne and prawn tails. The recipe makes 680 ml (1⅕ pints) of sauce.

Fondue de Tomate Portugaise
Portuguese Tomato Fondue

500 g (1 lb) tomatoes
50 g (2 oz) shallots
1½ dessertspoons butter
½ clove garlic, crushed
salt and pepper

1 medium-sized heavy saucepan
1 larger saucepan

Skin the tomatoes by dipping them in boiling water for a few seconds. Remove pips and chop. Chop shallots. (If shallots are unavailable, use very small onions or just the centre part of large onions.) Heat the butter in a heavy saucepan, add the shallots, the garlic and the tomatoes. Simmer slowly, stirring with a wooden spoon. When almost all the liquid has evaporated – a process the French call *reduire* or to reduce – add salt and pepper and keep warm if you wish over a saucepan of boiling water. Makes about 350 ml (⅗ pint) of fondue.

Sauce Raifort
Horseradish Sauce

SERVES 8

4 dessertspoons horseradish, grated
2 teaspoons vinegar
½ teaspoon powdered Colman's mustard
1 soupspoon fresh breadcrumbs
200 ml (⅓ pint) fresh cream
½ teaspoon icing sugar
salt and pepper
5 drops Worcestershire sauce

1 mixing bowl
1 whisk

Mix the horseradish, vinegar, mustard and breadcrumbs in a bowl, add the cream gradually, then add the sugar, salt and pepper and Worcestershire sauce. Beat and serve.

Sauce Rémoulade
Rémoulade Sauce

30 g (1 oz) gherkins, chopped
30 g (1 oz) capers, chopped
parsley and chervil, freshly minced
1 fillet of anchovy, finely chopped, or anchovy paste
250 ml (scant ½ pint) mayonnaise (page 124)

1 mixing bowl

Incorporate the gherkins, capers, herbs and anchovies into a mayonnaise (page 124). This makes 350 ml (⅗ pint) of sauce.

Sauce Smitane
Smitane Sauce

ENOUGH FOR 8
4 dessertspoons white onions,
  chopped
50 g (1¾ oz) fresh butter
150 ml (¼ pint) dry white wine
500 ml (scant pint) sour cream
  (page 47)
salt and freshly-ground pepper
1 teaspoon lemon juice

1 heavy-bottomed pan

Toss the onions in the butter until golden, then add the wine and simmer to reduce until the liquid just covers the bottom of the pan. Remove and add the sour cream, a pinch of salt, freshly-ground pepper and the lemon juice. Stir and serve.

You can put this sauce through a sieve if you wish to remove the onions. It is a matter of taste.

Sauce Tartare
Tartar Sauce

The classic French recipe for a *sauce tartare* is a mayonnaise using hard-boiled eggs. The pounded yolks of three hard-boiled eggs replace the egg yolks in the master recipe for mayonnaise (page 124) and chopped pickles and herbs are added as in the Sauce Rémoulade (page 127). You can add a little beaten cream or the stiffly beaten whites of 2 eggs, or the sieved whites of 2 hard-boiled eggs.

Sauce Verte
Green Sauce

100 g (3½ oz) mixed spinach,
  watercress, tarragon, chives
  and chervil

Cook all the ingredients in boiling water for 6–7 minutes. Blend in the liquidizer (or put through a food mill or strainer), then strain through a cheesecloth to remove all the water.

Make a mayonnaise (page 124), and then carefully add the liquidized vegetables. Check the seasoning, and if the sauce is

1 pan boiling water
1 liquidizer
1 strainer
1 cheesecloth

too thick add a little tepid water. The sauce should be liquid enough to coat the eggs. Makes 600 ml (generous pint).

We use the *sauce verte* a lot. It accompanies fish, mousses and eggs. It is both pretty, as it has a pale green colour, and very light.

Sauce Caramel
Caramel Sauce

SERVES 8
3 dessertspoons golden syrup
3 dessertspoons honey
1 dessertspoon rum
pinch of vanilla powder (or ½ teaspoon vanilla essence)
3 dessertspoons fresh cream

1 heavy-bottomed pan to fit in *bain-marie*

The chef serves this sauce with the St James Biscuit.

Gently heat all ingredients except the cream in a heavy-bottomed pan. Allow to cool a little and then add the cream. Reheat in double boiler and serve hot.

By adding 3 dessertspoons butter and 3 dessertspoons brown sugar to the above you will obtain a butterscotch sauce.

Sauce au Chocolat
Chocolate Sauce

250 g (9 oz) bitter chocolate
100 g (3½ oz) butter
50 g (1¾ oz) castor sugar
2 dessertspoons brandy or rum
pinch vanilla powder

1 heavy pan to fit in *bain-marie*
1 whisk

Heat all ingredients, preferably in a *bain-marie*, stir and serve. We sometimes use cream instead of butter. This makes enough sauce to serve with a dessert for 8 people.

For a chocolate nut sauce served with Gâteau aux Noix Ambassadrice, page 154:

Add 2 dessertspoons chopped walnuts to the chocolate sauce. If it is too thick, add a little cream or more rum, depending on taste.

Beurre au Cognac
Brandy Butter

SERVES 6
200 g (7 oz) butter
100 g (3½ oz) icing sugar
100 ml (⅕ pint) brandy

1 mixing bowl
1 whisk or mixer

Beat the butter until it is white and light, add the sugar slowly, beating all the time. (I do this in the mixer.) Finally, gradually add the brandy. Keep the sauce in the refrigerator until you wish to serve it. The chef's advice is that the operation should be done in a 'tepid atmosphere', so that the butter is neither too hard nor too soft. If it is hard you cannot incorporate the sugar and if it is too soft it separates and does not become light. A good mixer, however, makes the process easier.

Note: If the sauce curdles, gently heat it in a *bain-marie* and, when tepid, beat it briskly, then cool and keep in the refrigerator.

Sauce Framboise
Raspberry Sauce

SERVES 6
400 g (14 oz) raspberries
juice of ½ small lemon
150 g (5 oz) castor sugar
pinch vanilla powder

1 liquidizer
1 sieve

Put all the ingredients in a liquidizer, and then through a fine sieve or strainer. It is best to make this sauce about 2 hours before serving, because it sets a little when left in the refrigerator and takes on a richer consistency.

Sauce aux Fruits
Fruit Sauce

This sauce can be made with any soft fruits you may be using.

250 g (9 oz) fruit
100 g (3½ oz) castor sugar
juice of ½ lemon

1 liquidizer
1 fine strainer

Blend all the ingredients in a liquidizer and then put it through a fine strainer before serving. You can add a liqueur if you wish; this is a matter of taste. These quantities will make enough for one sauceboat.

Sauce Gingembre
Ginger Sauce

200 ml (⅓ pint) golden syrup
200 ml (⅓ pint) ginger syrup
200 ml (⅓ pint) rum
50 g (1¾ oz) stem ginger, diced

1 heavy-bottomed pan

Heat the ingredients together and serve.

Note: for ginger syrup we use the syrup in the stem ginger jar. The golden syrup can be replaced by syrup at 22° density (page 180).

Another method which the chef uses with ginger pancakes is to bring to the boil 5 dessertspoons golden syrup, 3 dessertspoons water, 1 dessertspoon rum, 3 dessertspoons stem ginger (diced), and 3 dessertspoons castor sugar, boil together for a few seconds, and serve.

'Milord the swell' at the patisserie

LES DESSERTS

DESSERTS

Burnt Apricots	Abricots Brulés
Apricot Snow	Neige d'Abricots
Figs Princess	Figues Princesse
Iced Fig Gâteau	Gâteau de Figues Glacées
Strawberry Biscuit with Raspberry Sauce	Fraisier Sauce Framboise
Greek Orange Compote	Compote d'Orange à la Grecque
Orange Salad	Salade d'Oranges
Pineapple Marie	Ananas Marie
Apricot Ice	Glace aux Abricots
Ice Cream Elizabeth	Glace Elizabeth
Strawberry Ice	Glace aux Fraises
Gladstone Ice Cream	Glace Gladstone
Lychee Sorbet	Sorbet aux Lychees
Williamine Pear	Poire Williamine
Coffee Ice Cream Gâteau	Gâteau de Glace Moka
St James' Biscuit	Biscuit St James
Iced Praliné Soufflé	Soufflé Glacé Praliné
Iced Soufflé Alexandra	Soufflé Glacé Alexandra
Brandy Snaps	Brandy Snaps
Ambassadress' Nut Gâteau	Gâteau aux Noix Ambassadrice
Moor in a Shirt	Nègre en Chemise
Guard's Pudding	Guard's Pudding
Ginger Pudding	Pudding au Gingembre
Raspberry Tarts	Tartes aux Framboises
Mince Pies	Mince Pies
Christmas Pudding	Pudding de Noël
Apple Pie with Cheddar	Pie de Pommes au Cheddar
Mademoiselle Tatin's Tart	Tarte de Mademoiselle Tatin
Treacle Tarts	Tartelettes au Golden Syrup
Ginger Pancakes	Crêpes au Gingembre
Cardinal Meringues	Meringues Cardinales
Cambridge Trifle	Trifle de Cambridge
Cream Heart	Coeur à la Crème
Avocado Mousse	Mousse d'Avocats
Mont Blanc	Mont Blanc
Lemon Posset	Lemon Posset

Abricots Brulés
Burnt Apricots

This is one of my daughter's favourite dishes. She makes it in London for her friends because it is easy to make and can be prepared in advance.

SERVES 6–8

600 g (1 lb 5 oz) dried apricots
500 g (1 lb 2 oz) cooking apples
200 g (7 oz) granulated sugar
juice of 1 lemon
200 g (7 oz) brown sugar

1 bowl of cold water
1 medium-sized pan with lid
1 heavy medium-sized pan with lid
1 fine sieve
1 30-cm (12-in) oval baking dish
1 spatula

Soak the apricots in cold water for 2 hours, strain and then put them in a pan with water to cover. Cook, covered, for 30 minutes over a gentle heat.

Meanwhile peel, quarter and core the apples. Put them in a heavy pan with 150 ml (¼ pint) water and the granulated sugar. Cover and cook gently for 20 minutes. When the apples and apricots are cooked put them through a fine sieve, mix with the lemon juice and arrange in the baking dish. Pass a spatula over the dish when it is full to obtain a flat surface, and allow it to cool. When cold, scatter a layer of brown sugar over the apricot–apple mixture and put the dish under the grill or in a very hot oven so that the sugar melts into a brown caramel. Repeat the layers of sugar, returning the dish to the grill or oven each time, until you have used all the sugar. You should then have a hard layer of almost black caramel. Allow to cool, then serve with a bowl of fresh whipped cream.

Neige d'Abricots

Apricot Snow

This is a light and unusual dessert. It is easy to make and looks pretty. We serve it for small dinners and my daughter likes making it in London for her friends.

SERVES 6

4 lumps sugar
whites of 6 eggs
pinch salt
750 g (1½ lb) apricot jam
few toasted almonds
few crystallized apricots
2 dessertspoons rum

1 small heavy-bottomed pan
1 pudding basin or china mould
   17.5 cm (7 in) in diameter
1 mixing bowl
1 whisk
1 spatula
1 double boiler for *bain-marie*

Heat the sugar with 2 dessertspoons water and make a caramel, i.e. let the sugar boil until it turns brown (page 180). Pour the caramel into the pudding basin. Beat the egg whites with a pinch of salt until firm. Beat 500 g (1 lb) apricot jam and carefully fold it into the egg whites with a spatula. Put this mixture into the pudding basin, cover and cook in a pan half-filled with boiling water (a *bain-marie*) in a moderate oven, 200 °C (400 °F)/Mark 6, for 30 minutes. Uncover and allow to cool. Turn out on to a serving dish and decorate with almonds and crystallized apricots. Heat and then sieve the remaining apricot jam, mix it with the rum and allow to cool before serving as a separate sauce.

Figues Princesse
Figs Princess

This is a very elegant yet easy dessert. You can prepare it in advance and it looks more complicated than it is.

SERVES 8

16 large figs (or 24 medium-sized ones)
200 g (7 oz) castor sugar
150 ml (¼ pint) Grand Marnier
250 g (½ lb) fresh almonds
juice of 1 lemon
500 g (1 lb) fresh raspberries
100 ml (7 dessertspoons) fresh cream

2 mixing bowls
1 liquidizer
1 fine sieve

Peel the figs. Cut the tops of them into 4 without cutting right down to the base. Pull out the 4 points so that the pink flesh of the figs can be seen. Arrange the figs in a bowl and scatter half the sugar and all the Grand Marnier over them. Leave to macerate for 1 hour, scooping up the Grand Marnier and pouring it over the figs from time to time. Meanwhile peel and skin the almonds. Split them into halves and leave them in a bowl of water with the lemon juice so that they keep their colour.

Blend the raspberries and the remainder of the sugar in the liquidizer, and then put them through a fine sieve. Arrange the figs in a serving dish, and mix their macerating juices with the liquidized raspberry pulp. Push some of the almond halves into the figs. Pour over the liquidized raspberry pulp mixture. Scatter the remainder of the almond halves over the dish and decorate with fresh, beaten cream. Serve the rest of the raspberry pulp mixture in a sauceboat to accompany the dish.

Gâteau de Figues Glacées
Iced Fig Gâteau

This is a dish I picked up in Chile where the figs were plentiful, ripe and sweet. I served it in Spain, too, where figs were easy to buy. In Paris we have served the dish with success, but great care has to be taken to buy really ripe and juicy figs.

SERVES 8

1.5–2 kg (3½–4½ lb) fresh, ripe figs
9 heaped dessertspoons castor sugar
juice of 3–4 lemons
100 ml (⅙ pint) Grand Marnier
little whipped cream
few skinned almonds

1 22.5-cm (8-in) cake tin with removable rim
1 plate

Peel the figs and slice them across in halves. Pile them into the tin (wet it first and sprinkle it with some sugar), sprinkling each layer with 3 heaped tablespoons sugar and about 4 dessertspoons lemon juice. When the tin is full, press down very firmly on the contents, then weight it with a plate on top of the tin. Place in the freezer for at least 5 hours. When ready to serve, unmould on to a serving plate. Pour the Grand Marnier over it and decorate with cream and almonds if you wish.

If the cake is too hard, allow it to stand for a few minutes before serving. Our chef serves this dessert with a raspberry sauce (page 130).

Fraisier Sauce Framboise
Strawberry Biscuit with Raspberry Sauce

This is a pretty light French dessert. You can also use the recipe for making a raspberry biscuit with strawberry sauce.

SERVES 8

1 kg (2 lb) strawberries
300 ml (½ pint) fresh cream
150 ml (¼ pint) milk
100 g (3½ oz) castor sugar
1 teaspoon vanilla essence (or powdered vanilla)
raspberry sauce (page 130)
5 round 20-cm (8-in) biscuits (page 150)

1 bowl
1 whisk or mixer
1 icing bag with decorative nozzle

Wash the strawberries and drain them well. Remove stalks (always do this after washing them so as to prevent them from becoming soggy). Beat the cream and milk together until fairly stiff. Add the sugar and beat until stiff. If you are using powdered vanilla, mix it with the sugar; if you are using vanilla essence, add it to the cream and milk mixture.

Place one biscuit round on the serving dish and carefully arrange a layer of strawberries over it. With an icing bag full of the cream, decorate the gaps between the strawberries. Add another biscuit round, more strawberries and cream, etc. When you have placed the final biscuit round decorate the sides and the top with piped cream. Place a few strawberries on the top and round the dish. Pour over a little raspberry sauce, and serve the remainder separately in a sauceboat.

Note: In France fresh cream is very thick and that is why milk is added when beating. If your double cream is not too thick and just right for piping through an icing bag, use cream only. You will need 450 ml (¾ pint).

Compote d'Orange à la Grecque
Greek Orange Compote

A large bowl of orange compote is always a success. In Greece the oranges are plentiful and fresh off the trees. This recipe, which I have used in many Embassies, has a touch of originality and is very good. It can be prepared in advance and is even better that way.

SERVES 6–8

8–10 oranges
2 lemons
8–10 lumps sugar
3 dessertspoons rum or kirsch
500 g (1 lb 2 oz) sugar
4 cups water

1 heavy pan
1 earthenware or china bowl
1 heavy pan

Peel the oranges, retaining the peel of four of them. Slice this peel very thinly in strips, removing all white inner skin. Boil strips for 1 minute in a little water and drain. Slice the oranges, having carefully removed all the white skin and pith. Remove pips and place the slices in the bowl. Rub lumps of sugar over the lemon peel, and place these under the layer of orange slices, then pour on the juice of the lemons. Heat the sugar water and orange rinds in a heavy saucepan. Use less sugar if the oranges are very sweet. Boil until a sugar thread is formed when you dip a spoon into the syrup and lift it out. Pour this syrup over the orange slices. Leave covered overnight in the refrigerator. Next day add rum or kirsch and, if you wish, decorate with walnuts. Serve very cold.

Salade d'Oranges
Orange Salad

The presentation of this orange salad is beautiful and original. The oranges appear in a glass bowl covered with a net of burnt sugar. When we served this dish at a lunch for the Comédie Française, the actors and the director, Monsieur Dux, liked the crunchy sugar so much that conversation stopped quite a while.

SERVES 6–8

8 oranges
4 dessertspoons castor sugar
1 wineglass Drambuie or Grand Marnier
200 g (7 oz) lump sugar

cocktail sticks
1 heavy, preferably copper, pan
greaseproof paper

Carefully peel the oranges and cut them in round slices. Put them back in their original shape and secure them with the cocktail sticks. Place them in the serving bowl and scatter the castor sugar over them. (The amount will vary according to how sweet the oranges are.) Pour over the Drambuie or Grand Marnier. Scoop up this juice and baste the oranges with it several times.

In the copper pan heat the lump sugar until it has reached the caramel stage (page 180). Then take a spoonful of the caramel and pour it on to a sheet of oiled greaseproof paper, making it flow downwards and then across. Repeat with the rest of the caramel so that you get a kind of pattern – described by the chef as looking like a fisherman's net. Break the sugar net into large pieces and decorate the oranges with it. The chef places the pieces upright and across the dish. It is very decorative.

Ananas Marie
Pineapple Marie

Perhaps it is as obvious to my readers as no doubt it has been to our guests that I like ginger. The usual pineapple surprise can be good if it is very freshly made, but our version is prettier and more original. As it was my invention the chef has given it my name. The chef serves the pineapple halves in gondolas of twisted starched napkins. You can also serve them in a nest of spun sugar (see page 182) or on a bed of decorative leaves. The chef sometimes trims the pineapple leaves to make them prettier; he also rubs the pineapples with a little oil so that the shells shine.

SERVES 8

4 pineapples, each weighing about 500 g (1 lb)

550 ml (1 pint) syrup at 22° (page 180)

juice of 1 lemon

white of 1 egg

600 g (1 lb 5 oz) lychees, tinned

100 g (3½ oz) stem ginger, very thinly sliced

1 grapefruit knife
1 spoon
1 liquidizer
1 strainer
1 ice cream churn

Cut each pineapple in half lengthwise, so that you halve the green leaves. Carefully remove the flesh, using a grapefruit knife and a spoon. Remove the hard centre and blend the pulp in the liquidizer with the syrup. Strain the pineapple mixture, together with the lemon juice and the egg white into an ice cream churn. Turn for about 20 minutes. When hard, arrange little balls (using an ice cream ladle or teaspoon) in the pineapple shell. Place the lychees over these and scatter over the thinly sliced (*julienne*) ginger.

If you cannot find small pineapples you can serve one large one cut in two. We serve a hot ginger sauce and brandy snaps with this dish (pages 131 and 153).

Glace aux Abricots
Apricot Ice

The chef's fruit ices are light and fresh, and to make them successfully you do need a pèse-sirop or saccharometer. It makes the process easier and more accurate. When we serve fruit ices we try either to serve the same fruit in small tarts to accompany the ice or we incorporate the diced crystallized fruit to give the ice a stronger flavour.

SERVES 6–8

550 ml (1 pint) syrup boiled to
   32° density (see method)
500 g (1 lb) apricots
juice of 1 lemon
100 g (3½ oz) fresh cream
100 g (3½ oz) crystallized apricots,
   diced

1 heavy pan for syrup
1 *pèse-sirop*
1 saucepan
1 fine sieve
1 mixing bowl
1 ice churn or sorbet churn
1 chilled mould or bomb
1 spatula

Make the syrup by boiling 500 g (1 lb) loaf or lump sugar in 250 ml (scant ½ pint) water. Use a *pèse-sirop* to measure density; it should yield 550 ml (1 pint) of syrup at 32° (page 180).

Lightly poach the apricots in boiling water for 5 minutes, drain, and push them through a fine sieve into a bowl. Add the lemon juice and the syrup. Add water until the mixture registers 19° on the *pèse-sirop*. Pour into the churn and turn for 20–30 minutes.

When the ice has thickened press it into a chilled mould with a spatula, and freeze for 3 hours. Then turn the mould upside down and scoop a hole in the centre of the ice. Fill this with a mixture of cream and the crystallized apricots and 'shut' the hole with a layer of the ice you have cut out. Replace the ice in the freezer until you wish to serve it. Leave for at least 20 minutes.

Just before serving dip the mould or bomb into hot water and unmould on to a serving dish. The chef unmoulds his ices on to folded napkins to prevent their slipping on the dish. He decorates the ice with more cream and crystallized apricots. He prefers to serve the ices in 'homemade' sugar dishes (page 204), and he serves this ice with small almond balls (*boules d'amandes*).

For the almond balls:
200 g (7 oz) icing sugar
200 g (7 oz) ground almonds
yolks of 6 eggs
2 drops almond essence
drop food colouring (green)
white of 1 egg, beaten
100 g (3½ oz) castor sugar

1 mixing bowl

For the almond balls:

Put the icing sugar, ground almonds, egg yolks, almond essence and colouring in a bowl. Mix well. Make into small balls weighing about 10 g (⅓ oz). Dip them into the egg white and then the castor sugar and leave them to dry out. You can serve them in a little dish separately or in a small 'homemade' sugar dish (page 204).

Glace Elizabeth
Ice Cream Elizabeth

Basically this is a cherry ice with a cream and candied cherry filling, served with tiny fruit tarts. We like serving fruit ice creams with small tarts that include the same fruit. Black cherries are ideal for this and make a delicious summer sweet.

SERVES 6–8

550 ml (1 pint) syrup boiled to
    32° density (see method and
    page 180)
800 g (scant 2 lb) black cherries
pinch cinnamon
juice of ½ lemon
40 ml (3 dessertspoons) kirsch
1 dessertspoon castor sugar
200 g (7 oz) fresh double cream
12 4-cm (1½-in) tart shells

1 heavy pan for syrup
1 *pèse-sirop*
1 mortar
1 fine strainer
1 small heavy pan
1 ice cream churn
1 ice cream bomb or mould

Make the syrup by boiling 500 g (1 lb) loaf or lump sugar in 250 ml (scant ½ pint) water. Use a *pèse-sirop* to measure density.

Stone the cherries, then pound half the stones in a mortar and boil them with the syrup. Strain through a fine strainer. Poach the cherries in the strained syrup, add the cinnamon, lemon juice and kirsch. Remove half the cherries and put them through a fine sieve; add three-quarters of the syrup and a little water to bring the density to 19° (page 180). Pour this mixture into the ice cream churn and turn until stiff. Simmer the remainder of the cherries in the remainder of the syrup until they are candied. When the ice cream is stiff, press into the bomb mould, leaving a well in the centre (roughly one-quarter of the total volume of the ice) and place it in the freezer for at least 3 hours. (You can, if you wish, fill your mould and proceed as for Strawberry Ice (page 144), scooping out a well later.)

At the end of the freezing time, add the sugar to the cream, beat well, and divide mixture into two. The chef then removes the mould from the freezer as the first course is being served, takes half the beaten cream and mixes it with the candied cherries. He piles this mixture into the well in the ice cream and returns the bomb to the freezer for at least 20 minutes. Just before serving he dips the ice cream bomb in warm water, carefully unmoulds it on to a dish covered with a folded napkin and decorates the bomb with the rest of the cream, using a bag or syringe. He places his tiny tarts round the ice cream bomb and has some more – as they are very popular – which are handed round on a separate plate. If I were doing it myself, I would prepare the bomb and fill it well in advance. I daren't suggest this to Monsieur Viaëne as he, like all first-class chefs, believes that any mixing should be done at the last minute.

Glace aux Fraises
Strawberry Ice

This is very much like the apricot ice and, in fact, most fruit ices are made in the same way. The chef likes to leave the centre of his bomb empty for the first part of the freezing because he likes to pack freshly beaten cream mixed with crystallized fruits or praline almonds into this hole. But of course you do not need to do this. We also like to serve little tart shells filled with one large strawberry and covered with a little redcurrant jelly with this ice.

SERVES 6–8

550 ml (1 pint) syrup at 32°
    density (see method)
650 g (1½ lb) strawberries for pulp
juice of 1 orange
juice of 1 lemon
100 ml (⅛ pint) fresh cream
1 dessertspoon castor sugar
200 g (7 oz) fresh strawberries,
    chopped

1 heavy pan for syrup
1 *pèse-sirop*
1 fine sieve
1 ice cream churn
1 ice cream mould or bomb

Make the syrup by boiling 500 g (1 lb) loaf or lump sugar in 250 ml (scant ½ pint) water. Use a *pèse-sirop* to measure density; it should yield 550 ml (1 pint) of syrup at 32° (page 180). Crush the strawberries, then press them through a fine sieve. You will need 500 g (1 lb) pulp.

Mix the strawberry pulp with the syrup, then add the orange and lemon juices and a little water to bring the mixture to an ice cream density of 18° on the saccharometer or *pèse-sirop*. Pour the mixture into the churn and churn for about 20 minutes. Fill the ice cream mould and freeze for 3 hours at least. The chef then takes the mould out, scoops a hole in the centre of the ice, fills this with the cream beaten with the sugar and mixed with a few chopped strawberries. He closes the hole with a little of the ice cream mixture and returns the mould to the freezer for at least 20 minutes. To unmould, dip the mould into hot water for a few seconds and unmould on to a serving dish. Decorate with strawberries and more beaten cream. The chef has a folded napkin on his dish to avoid the ice slipping, or he makes a *génoise* base (page 179).

Glace Gladstone
Gladstone Ice Cream

The chef and I don't think that Gladstone ever tasted this ice but it is a combination that I like. It is easy to prepare and always pleases our guests. The chef decided to give it an English name.

SERVES 6–8
100 g (3½ oz) stem ginger
750 ml (1½ pints) vanilla ice (page 187)
200 g (7 oz) fresh cream
1 dessertspoon castor sugar

1 mixing bowl
1 1-litre (2-pint) ice cream mould

Chop three-quarters of the ginger into cubes, cut the rest into small triangles. Mix half the ginger cubes into the ice cream. Press the mixture into the mould, leaving an empty space in the centre. Put the mould into the freezer.

Beat the cream and add 1 dessertspoon castor sugar. Divide the cream in half. Mix the remainder of the ginger cubes into one half of the cream and spoon this into the centre of the ice cream mould when it is well frozen.

When you want to serve the ice cream, dip the mould into hot water up to the rim and turn out on to a dish covered with a folded napkin. You can, if you wish, serve this ice cream on a thin sponge layer or *génoise* which has been imbibed with rum (page 179).

Decorate with the triangular pieces of ginger and the remainder of the cream. We serve this ice cream with a ginger sauce which looks difficult but is very easy (page 131).

Sorbet aux Lychees
Lychee Sorbet

This is one of our favourite desserts. We serve it in the chef's flute-edged sugar bowls (page 204). Once when Mr Hillier, the famous garden expert, was our guest of honour for a garden exhibition we held in the Residence garden, I asked the chef to call it 'Sorbet Hillier' and we presented it in a trug which he made out of sugar. The chef filled his beautiful trug with little balls of the lychee sorbet scooped out with a round ice cream scoop, on top of which he arranged whole lychees. He decorated the edges and the spaces between the lychees with tiny flowers made out of marzipan. The guests applauded when the dessert was presented.

SERVES 6–8

550 ml (1 pint) syrup boiled to 32° density (see method)
500 g (1 lb) lychees
white of 1 egg
60 g (2 oz) castor sugar
juice of 1 large lemon

1 heavy pan for syrup
1 *pèse sirop*
1 liquidizer or sieve
1 double boiler
1 copper pan
1 ice cream churn
1 mixing bowl

Make the syrup by boiling 500 g (1 lb) loaf or lump sugar in 250 ml (scant ½ pint) water. Use a *pèse-sirop* or saccharometer to measure density; it should yield 550 ml (1 pint) of syrup at 32° (page 180).

Put the lychees in a liquidizer and blend, or crush them through a sieve. You will need 550 ml (1 pint) pulp.

Make Italian meringue from the egg white and castor sugar (page 186).

Mix the syrup, lychee pulp and lemon juice together and add water until the saccharometer measures 15° density. Pour the mixture into an ice cream churn and turn for about 25 minutes, then add the Italian meringue and mix well. Serve immediately or keep in the freezer. Serve in a deep dish and decorate with whole lychees and mint leaves if you wish.

Note: You can use these proportions to make any fruit sorbets you wish: cherry, pineapple, orange, tangerine, lemon, red-currant, raspberry and strawberry.

Poire Williamine
Williamine Pear

This is a delightful, light, original and beautiful sweet. We have served it on state occasions and once we served it at an important meeting between British businessmen and directors of Renault, whose latest car was being advertised as being the shape of a pear. They appreciated the compliment!

SERVES 6–8

For the sorbet:

4 large pears
500 ml (scant pint) syrup at 32° density (see method)
juice of 1 lemon
200 ml ($\frac{1}{3}$ pint) Poire Williamine liqueur

1 saucepan
1 liquidizer or sieve
1 heavy pan for syrup
1 *pèse-sirop*
1 mixing bowl
1 ice cream or sorbet churn

Poach the pears in water for 20 minutes, strain, and blend in a liquidizer or push through a sieve to purée. You will need 500 ml (scant pint) pulp.

Make the syrup by boiling 500 g (1 lb) loaf or lump sugar in 250 ml (scant $\frac{1}{2}$ pint) water. Use a *pèse-sirop* or saccharometer to measure density; it should yield 550 ml (1 pint) of syrup at 32° (page 180). Mix this with the pear purée, lemon juice, and the liqueur. Test with a saccharometer, adding water if necessary to obtain a mixture of 15°–17° density. Pour into a *sorbetière* or ice cream churn and turn for about 20 minutes. When the mixture is firm, turn out on your serving dish.

My chef turns it out on a dish which has a napkin folded on it (to prevent it from sliding). He then moulds it into the shape of a pear and puts it in the freezer. An hour later he paints it, using slightly caramelized sugar. (You can use a few drops of colouring or a few drops of caramel in the remains of your syrup, as it is not worth making a caramel for this purpose; you should have some left over, since the syrup recipe makes slightly more than you need for the ice.) He then puts it back in the freezer and about half an hour later he repeats the operation, this time using a deeper colour, that is to say, adding more colour or caramel. With this darker colour he shades his pear to make it look more real.

He decorates the base of his pear with green marzipan. Mix 150 g (5 oz) powdered almonds with 100 g (3$\frac{1}{2}$ oz) icing sugar and the yolks of 2 eggs. Add a few drops of green food colouring, then put the mixture through a sieve with large holes, cutting the marzipan with a knife as it comes through. This gives you a light green base to surround your golden pear.

Of course, you need not do all this. You can serve your

sorbet in a glass dish decorated with slices of cooked pear. We often serve the Poire Williamine liqueur as a sauce to accompany the pear sorbet.

PS. My chef is an artist. And he is not content with just a beautiful golden pear which has been painted twice! He likes to add a stalk and a leaf. You can add a fresh one if it is available, but I give you here his method for making one out of sugar – it is delicious and pretty.

250 g (9 oz) sugar (preferably lump)
½ dessertspoon glucose
100 ml (⅕ pint) water
green colouring
little oil

1 heavy pan, preferably copper
1 pastry brush
1 baking tin

Bring the sugar, glucose and water to the boil in a copper pan, stirring gently. Clean the rim of the saucepan, if necessary, with a brush dipped in cold water. Cover and boil until sugar has reached the large crack stage – that is to say when tested by dropping a little syrup in a cup of cold water, the sugar becomes hard and snaps easily but does not stick to the teeth (see notes on sugar, page 180). Remove the pan from the heat and pour the syrup into a baking tin. The chef switches on the oven (moderate heat) and places the baking tin on the oven door (which opens downwards) to keep the sugar warm and pliable. Add a little green food colouring and work with your fingers, mixing the colouring and pulling the sugar (your fingers should be slightly oiled). Pull out a piece for the stem of the pear. Pull out and mould the leaves. By pulling you can obtain a pointed leaf. Stick these to the stem by heating the ends over a flame, then allow to harden. Place stem and leaves on your pear before serving.

Gâteau de Glace Moka
Coffee Ice Cream Gâteau

This is a delicious and useful way of presenting ice cream. The coffee ice is sandwiched between two layers of light nut gâteau which is iced on top just like a cake. It looks pretty on buffets and can be made in advance.

SERVES 8

500 ml (scant pint) coffee ice cream (see method)
50 g (scant 2 oz) cornflour
60 g (2 oz) walnuts, chopped
60 g (2 oz) powdered almonds
180 g (generous 6 oz) castor sugar
1 small egg
3 eggs, separated

1 mixing bowl
1 mixer or whisk
1 15-cm (6-in) cake tin with removable rim
greaseproof paper
1 spatula
1 double-boiler

Make a coffee ice cream using the master recipe on page 187 and adding coffee essence to taste, or dissolve 2 generous dessertspoons Nescafé in the milk used in recipe.

Mix the cornflour, chopped walnuts, powdered almonds and sugar. Add the whole egg and the egg yolks, stir well and fold in the stiffly beaten whites. Arrange in the greased and floured cake tin and place in a moderately slow oven, 160 °C (325 °F)/Mark 3, for ¾–1 hour. Allow the cake to cool and cut in two across. Line the cake tin with greaseproof paper. Place one half of the nut cake in the bottom of the tin. Spoon in the coffee ice cream and cover with the other half of the cake. Leave in the freezer for at least 3 hours. Before serving, unmould on to a serving dish, pour a little chocolate sauce or icing (pages 129 and 184) over the cake and decorate with coffee grains, if you wish, or walnut halves. Return cake to freezer for a few minutes to allow the icing to harden.

Reheat any remaining sauce or icing in a double-boiler, adding 2 dessertspoons rum if you wish, and serve separately.

Biscuit St James
St James' Biscuit

This is the chef's invention. He first served it for Sir Christopher Soames (now Lord Soames) and Sir Christopher gave it the chef's name – and added the 'Saint'. It is a dish for a very grand party as it needs a great deal of preparation. But it is both ravishing to look at and delicious to eat. We have served it on many important state occasions and it has always been a success.

The biscuit is a layered tower, with each layer consisting of a different sorbet. You can choose any colour combination by varying your ingredients. (If you wish, of course, you can buy the different sorbets ready-made.) The chef uses pistachio, strawberry, lemon and raspberry sorbets.

SERVES 8

1 litre (2 pints) assorted sorbets
50 g (1¾ oz) butter, softened
125 g (4¼ oz) icing sugar, sifted
whites of 3 eggs
85 g (3 oz) flour, sifted
pinch vanilla powder

1 mixing bowl
1 mixer or whisk
1 or 2 baking trays, buttered
1 cake tin with removable rim,
    15 cm (6 in) in diameter and
    about 10 cm (4 in) high
1 spatula

Prepare your four different sorbets (page 146). You will need 250 ml (½ pint) of each one.

Beat the butter and sugar into a light cream. Continue beating and add the egg whites, flour and vanilla – very, very gradually, beating all the time. Take a heaped spoon of this mixture and arrange it on a buttered baking tray. Flatten it out with a spatula so that you have a round 'biscuit' about 15 cm (6 in) in diameter. Make 5 of these rounds. Cook in a preheated moderate oven, 200 °C (400 °F)/Mark 6, for 6–7 minutes. As soon as you remove the rounds from the oven, trim them carefully to fit the cake mould. Place one biscuit round on the base of the mould and start arranging the layers of sorbet in the mould. (You should have 4 layers of sorbet, with the round biscuits in between and ending with a biscuit.) This process must be done quickly so that the sorbets do not melt. Put in the freezer for at least 3 hours.

To serve, unmould on to a dish. (The chef places a folded napkin under the biscuit to prevent it from slipping.) You can ease the unmoulding by passing a knife round the mould. Serve with a fruit sauce (page 131) if you have used fruit sorbets. The chef serves a kind of butterscotch sauce (page 129).

Soufflé Glacé Praliné
Iced Praline Soufflé

This is a favourite soufflé. It is very popular at buffets and delights one's visiting god-children. The chef has a special way of serving it with transparent slices of brandy snaps wedged round the rim of the soufflé. And we serve with it a plate of brandy snaps, too. Our main idea in all this (and in all dishes) is to serve something with the sweet that recalls the main taste in the sweet – here the crunchy praliné is repeated in the crunchy brandy snaps. With fruit ices, the fruit is repeated in the tiny tarts. Sometimes for lunch parties we serve the praliné soufflé with an orange salad (page 140) with a network of burnt sugar – crunchy sugar recalls the praliné taste.

SERVES 8

250 g (8½ oz) sugar
100 g (3½ oz) almonds
yolks of 8 eggs
200 ml (⅓ pint) milk
500 ml (scant pint) fresh double
   cream, beaten

1 heavy pan, preferably copper
1 oiled marble slab
1 mixing bowl
1 mixer or whisk
1 *bain-marie*
1 fine sieve
1 17.5-cm (7-in) soufflé dish

Heat 100 g (3½ oz) sugar gradually in the copper pan and when it has taken on a deep golden caramel colour, add the almonds and stir. Turn out on to an oiled marble slab or heavy oven tin and allow to cool, then crush or grate finely. Beat the egg yolks with the remaining sugar until light and frothy. Heat up the milk and when it is boiling pour it over the frothy egg mixture, beating all the time. Continue beating over a gentle heat in a double boiler or *bain-marie*, to thicken. Then add the praliné almonds. Cool and strain through a fine sieve. Fold the cream into the mixture. Carefully fill the prepared (page 35) soufflé dish. Put it in the freezer for at least 6 hours. Just before serving, remove the paper collar from the soufflé dish and decorate it, if you wish, with either praliné almonds (page 182) or thin slices of flat brandy snaps poked round the soufflé in the shape of a crown.

Soufflé Glacé Alexandra
Iced Soufflé Alexandra

This soufflé is an adaptation of a caramel soufflé. It was my idea and the chef has given it my daughter's name — she is a keen cook, too.

SERVES 8

whites of 6 eggs
250 g (9 oz) sugar
400 ml (⅔ pint) *crème anglaise* or custard (page 187)
400 ml (⅔ pint) cream, beaten
500 g (1 lb 2 oz) lychees

1 17.5-cm (7-in) soufflé dish
kitchen paper or foil
string
1 mixing bowl
1 mixer or whisk
1 heavy saucepan

Prepare the soufflé dish with a collar of kitchen paper or foil tied with string (page 35).

Beat the egg whites until they are very firm. Make a caramel by boiling the sugar with 1 dessertspoon water; it's best to use lump sugar. (See method on page 181.) Pour the hot caramel over the egg, beating continually so as to dissolve the caramel (this can be done in a mixer). Allow the mixture to get cold, then add the *crème anglaise* and the beaten cream. Pour into the prepared soufflé dish and place it in a cold refrigerator for at least 5 hours.

Ten minutes before serving, cut out a well in the centre of the soufflé with a spoon. Spoon in the lychees, cover up the hole with a little of the soufflé mixture and decorate with praliné almonds if you wish (page 182).

Before serving, remove the paper and tie a napkin round the dish, or stand the dish on a napkin to make serving easier. We serve a ginger sauce with the soufflé (page 131).

Brandy Snaps

A plate of brandy snaps served with the caramel soufflé is an excellent touch. We have also served brandy snaps on large buffets, placing them next to the iced soufflés, and they have always been a tremendous success.

MAKES ABOUT 40
100 g (3½ oz) clarified butter
100 g (3½ oz) demerara sugar
100 g (3½ oz) golden syrup
2 drops vanilla essence
100 g (3½ oz) flour
1 teaspoon powdered ginger
pinch salt
250 g (9 oz) cream, whipped

2 heavy-bottomed pans
1 fine sieve
1 greased baking tin
1 palette knife
1 wooden spoon or spatula
1 icing syringe or bag

Clarify the butter by melting it, heating it gently until the bubbles disappear, and then straining it through a fine sieve.

Heat the clarified butter with the sugar and golden syrup in a heavy-bottomed saucepan. Allow it to cool, then add the vanilla, lemon juice and flour sieved with the ginger and salt. Take spoonfuls of the mixture and make them into small, even-sized balls. Flatten them out on a greased baking tin, allowing room for spreading. They should be flat, thin and circular.

Cook until golden brown for 8–10 minutes in a moderate oven, 160 °C (325 °F)/Mark 3. Allow to cool a little, then lift gently with a palette knife and roll them round the greased handle of a wooden spoon or spatula to make them into little brown tubes. Fill them with whipped cream, pressed through with an icing syringe, just before serving.

My chef keeps the brandy snap mixture in the freezer in a large ball, and he uses it when he needs it. In England the mixture is usually spooned directly on the trays (allowing space for spreading), but the chef's method produces thinner brandy snaps that are all the same size.

Gâteau aux Noix Ambassadrice
Ambassadress' Nut Gâteau

This has been described by my daughter as 'disgustingly good'. And it really is. It is also easy to make and to store. It was given to me by a former French Ambassadress, Comtesse de Rose, and I am forever grateful to her for the recipe.

SERVES 8

225 g (½ lb) butter
225 g (½ lb) icing sugar
225 g (½ lb) almonds or walnuts, chopped
200 ml (⅓ pint) milk
1 vanilla pod
yolks of 3 eggs
about 12 sponge fingers

1 electric mixer
1 medium-sized pan
1 large pan of boiling water for bain-mairie
1 pudding mould

Beat the butter, sugar and nuts in an electric mixer for ½ hour. The more you beat this mixture the lighter it becomes. Make a custard by boiling the milk with the vanilla pod. Remove from the fire and add the egg yolks one by one, beating all the time. Return the custard to the fire, preferably in a double boiler or *bain-marie*, and beat until the mixture thickens. Allow custard to cool, then very gradually incorporate this custard or *crème anglaise* into the butter–nut mixture and beat the whole mixture for a further ½ hour. Arrange the sponge fingers around the sides and on the bottom of a pudding mould (we use a kugelhopf mould) and pour in the mixture. Place a layer of sponge fingers on the top and refrigerate. This gâteau is all the better for being made in advance.

Note: We serve a chocolate nut sauce (page 129) with this in winter and pour a little on the gâteau when serving. In the summer we pour over a fruit sauce (page 131) and use almonds instead of walnuts.

Negre en Chemise
Moor in a Shirt

This is an Austrian dish. It is an excellent dessert to serve in the winter when ices and sorbets are less suitable, and makes a delicious if rather rich pudding and a change from English puddings.

SERVES 8

120 g (4 oz) butter
5 eggs, separated
120 g (4 oz) icing sugar
250 g (½ lb) bitter chocolate, grated
250 g (½ lb) walnuts or almonds, finely grated
1 dessertspoon castor sugar
4 dessertspoons rum
soft white icing (page 183) or whipped cream

1 mixing bowl
1 mixer or whisk
1 greased pudding mould (see note)
1 large pan for steaming
1 spatula

Beat the butter until very light. Add egg yolks and icing sugar and beat again. Add the grated chocolate. Whisk the egg whites and gently fold these into the mixture with the grated almonds or walnuts. Have a pudding mould ready, greased and dusted with castor sugar. Pour the mixture in and steam or boil for 1 hour. Unmould, and before serving pour over rum and quickly cover with soft icing, using a spatula. Serve hot and pass round cream or icing in a sauceboat if you wish.

Note: The correct Austrian mould is like a kugelhopf tin with a centre hole or partition (this is filled with cream or icing when the pudding is unmoulded). It has a screw lid to prevent steam and water entering. A pudding mould covered with grease-proof paper or foil can be used if care is taken to avoid water entering the mould during cooking.

Guard's Pudding

This English nursery pudding, originally served to the Guards in the late nineteenth century, was always a great success in Paris. I first had it in France at Baronne Loulou de Waldner's romantic house, Mortefontaine – where Pauline, Napoleon's favourite sister, secretly wed Borghese before the official minimum time of widowhood was up. The dessert is also known as nanny's recipe.

SERVES 8

175 g (6 oz) butter
175 g (6 oz) castor sugar
175 g (6 oz) fresh breadcrumbs
3 eggs
3 dessertspoons thick strawberry jam
½ teaspoon bicarbonate of soda

1 mixing bowl
1 mixer or whisk
1 pudding basin
greaseproof paper or foil
string
1 *bain-marie*

Cream the butter and sugar until light, then add the breadcrumbs, well-beaten eggs, jam and the soda dissolved in a dessertspoon of tepid water. Mix well and put into a buttered pudding basin, leaving room for the mixture to swell and rise. Cover with buttered paper or foil tied round the bowl with a piece of string and steam in a double boiler or *bain-marie* for 2 hours. Turn out on a heated serving dish and serve hot, accompanied by hot strawberry jam sauce (we add a dash of rum to this), *crème anglaise* (page 187) or fresh cream. My chef adds a French touch to this very English pudding – he scatters a crown of praliné almonds (page 182) round the pudding.

Pudding au Gingembre
Ginger Pudding

This pudding and Guard's Pudding are very much our 'Pudding Maison'. We serve them for small dinners and large lunch parties. The chef decorates them by standing them in a ring of toasted almonds. Our French guests love them and our English guests are interested to see what a French chef does to a nursery pudding. I am glad to say that they bear no resemblance to school puddings.

SERVES 6–8

3 large eggs, separated
pinch salt
250 g (9 oz) flour, sifted
1 teaspoon bicarbonate of soda
2 teaspoons ground ginger
175 g (6 oz) sugar
140 g (5 oz) butter
3 dessertspoons golden syrup
250 ml (scant ½ pint) tepid milk
little crystallized ginger, chopped
   (optional)

1 mixing bowl
1 mixer or whisk
1 sieve
1 *bain-marie*
1 small pan for milk
1 spatula
1 pudding basin or charlotte tin
1 large pan for steaming

Stiffly beat the egg whites with a pinch of salt. Sieve the flour together with the bicarbonate of soda and ground ginger. Put the sugar and butter in a pan over some hot water (*bain-marie*) and stir until the mixture has melted and is no longer gritty. Add the egg yolks and beat for about 4 minutes. The mixture should be lukewarm. Remove from the heat and beat again for a few minutes. (If you have an electric mixer, turn into a mixer bowl and beat at high speed for a few minutes.)

Dissolve the golden syrup in the milk and add this to the egg mixture, stirring it in gradually. Then blend in the flour and mix carefully and well, preferably with a wooden spoon or rubber spatula. Finally, add the stiffly-beaten whites, folding them in lightly with a spatula. Grease a pudding basin or charlotte tin (we use a kugelhopf mould) and sprinkle a little chopped ginger on the bottom. Pour in the mixture, cover and steam for 2 hours. (The tin or mould should be only three-quarters full.)

Unmould on a warm serving dish and accompany with ginger sauce (page 131).

Note: If you do not have golden syrup, use ginger marmalade. Strain 3 dessertspoons through a fine sieve and reserve the fruit to use, chopped, instead of the crystallized ginger. You could of course use orange marmalade instead.

Tartes aux Framboises
Raspberry Tarts

Fruit tart is a traditional French dessert. The chef's tarts are light, and we often make individual medium-sized ones for small dinner parties.

SERVES 8

400 g (14 oz) pastry (pages 175 and 178)
150 ml (¼ pint) raspberry jelly
1 kg (2 lb) fresh raspberries
100 g (3½ oz) fresh cream

1 25-cm (10-in) tart or flan tin
greaseproof paper
dried white beans

Line the greased tart tin with pastry and pinch the edges. Prick the base of the tart with a fork and cover with a round piece of greaseproof paper and dried white beans. Bake the tart in a moderate oven, 200 °C (400 °F)/Mark 6, for 15 minutes. Take out, remove the paper and beans and put back in the oven at 150 °C (300 °F)/Mark 2 until the tart is cooked. Leave to cool, then unmould.

Gently heat the raspberry jelly and stir until it is tepid (you can also use redcurrant jelly). Fill the tart with the jelly and place the raspberries on top of this. Decorate with fresh cream if you wish, and serve.

Mince Pies

We serve these at Christmas parties, as is traditional, but we also make them throughout the year and include them in our little 'petits fours'. They are always a great success.

MAKES ABOUT 40

50 g (1¾ oz) beef suet
90 g (3 oz) brown sugar
50 g (1¾ oz) currants
50 g (1¾ oz) sultanas
50 g (1¾ oz) raisins, stoned
50 g (1¾ oz) cooking apples, chopped
30 g (1 oz) mixed candied peel, diced (mainly orange and lemon)
5 g (1 teaspoon) mixed spices: ginger, cloves and cinnamon
grated rind of 1 lemon
150 ml (¼ pint) Madeira
150 ml (¼ pint) brandy
shortcrust or rough puff pastry

1 mixing bowl
1 glass preserving jar with hermetically sealed top

Mix all the dry ingredients and then mince them. (You can add 30 g (1 oz) chopped almonds if you wish.) Pour over the Madeira and brandy. Mix well and spoon into a glass preserving jar. Seal, and allow to macerate for at least 3 weeks. Use when needed.

To make the pies, roll out 300 g (10 oz) shortcrust pastry or rough puff pastry (pages 178 and 176). The chef leaves it about 3 mm (⅛ in) thick. He then presses the pastry into tiny moulds, 4 cm (1½ in) in diameter. He fills the moulds with the mincemeat and covers the tarts with a little pastry which he presses down well round the edges on his fingers (he wets his fingers first). He pricks a small hole in the centre of each tart and cooks them for 15 minutes in a preheated moderate oven, 200 °C (400 °F)/Mark 6. Before serving he scatters castor sugar over the tarts. This quantity of pastry should give you 40 small mince pies.

Pudding de Noël
Christmas Pudding

I like to make my own plum puddings and I like to serve them at times other than Christmas. Some years ago I served them in the middle of a hot Chilean summer, at a large buffet supper-dance we gave for Princess Marina of Kent and Princess Alexandra in our garden in Santiago. The cold puddings were sliced and served with a light, creamy vanilla ice. We served them once in Paris for our November Jubilee Ball and Fashion Show. The head butler, Giovanni, led the procession carrying a rum and vanilla ice cream gâteau, topped by a gorgeous crown the chef had made out of sugar; behind him came the waiters, each carrying a traditional flaming plum pudding. The 250 guests applauded.

I had my favourite recipe for this traditional dish and the chef had collected others from his previous employers. One he preferred came from the Duchess of Windsor. We combined our recipes and this is the one we now use.

SERVES 6–8

200 g (7 oz) currants
100 g (3½ oz) sultanas, washed and dried
100 g (3½ oz) raisins, stoned and halved
75 g (2½ oz) fresh white breadcrumbs
75 g (2½ oz) flour, sifted
75 g (2½ oz) brown sugar
50 g (1¾ oz) carrots, grated
40 g (1½ oz) walnuts, chopped
35 g (1¼ oz) candied orange peel, diced
35 g (1¼ oz) candied lemon peel, diced
10 g (1 teaspoon) bitter almonds, chopped
3 g (½ teaspoon) salt
5 g (1 teaspoon) mixed spices: ginger, cinnamon, cloves, nutmeg
75 g (2½ oz) beef suet
2 eggs, lightly beaten
250 ml (scant ½ pint) beer
250 ml (scant ½ pint) brandy

1 large mixing bowl
1 20-cm (8-in) pudding basin
greaseproof paper or foil
1 pudding cloth
string
1 large pan with lid

Thoroughly mix all the dry ingredients. Then add the beef suet, eggs, beer and brandy. Cover the bowl and leave it to stand in a cool place for 2 days. Mix again and pour into a buttered pudding basin. Cover with a piece of greaseproof paper or foil. Tie a large cloth over this, lying the cloth flat over the top of the basin, tying it round the rim with string, and then tying the ends over the top in a knot. Boil or steam the pudding in a large covered pan of boiling water for 6 hours. Remove and allow to cool. When the pudding is completely cold, wrap the basin in foil. Keep in a cool place until needed. Plum puddings should be prepared well in advance. In the old days they were prepared almost a year ahead.

Before serving, boil or steam for another 3 hours. Unmould on to a deep heated dish. Heat 200 ml (⅓ pint) brandy, pour it over the pudding and set alight before serving. At Christmas, place a sprig of holly in the centre of the pudding. The chef also puts holly round the dish and this increases the flames around the pudding. We serve the pudding with brandy butter (page 130) at Christmas time and with vanilla ice or Gladstone ice (page 145) on other occasions.

Pie de Pommes au Cheddar
Apple Pie with Cheddar

There are many variations of the traditional British apple pie – this is the one I prefer. We do vary it sometimes by brushing the top with cinnamon (over the egg and milk glaze) or grated Cheddar cheese. The taste varies, too, when different types of apples are used. Cooking apples or reinettes are really best, though we have used Cox's and their sweetness gave an exceptionally good flavour.

SERVES 6–8

1 kg (2 lb) cooking apples
1 large quince
juice of 2 lemons
120–180 g (4–6 oz) brown sugar
½ teaspoon cinnamon
½ teaspoon nutmeg, grated
4 cloves
3 dessertspoons currants
4 dessertspoons sultanas
pinch salt
grated rind of 1 lemon
grated rind of ½ orange
juice of 1 orange
5 dessertspoons water
2 dessertspoons butter
500 g (1 lb) shortcrust pastry
    (page 178)
yolk of 1 egg
2 dessertspoons milk

1 large bowl
1 25-cm (10-in) oval pie dish
1 pastry brush

Peel, core and quarter the apples and the quince, or slice them thickly. Leave in a bowl of cold water with the juice of 1 lemon to keep their colour. Line the bottom of a buttered pie dish with the apple slices. Mix the sugar, spices, dried fruits, salt and lemon and orange rind. (The amount of sugar depends on the sweetness of the apples.) Sprinkle this mixture over the apples and quince in the pie dish, and then add alternate layers of apples and quince and the dry mixture until the dish is full. Place an inverted egg cup or a pie funnel in the centre of the dish. Pour in the remaining lemon juice, the orange juice and the water. Dot with butter and cover with pastry crust.

For the crust, roll out the pastry and first cut a narrow strip. Wet the rim of the pie dish with cold water, and press down the strip around it. From the remainder of the pastry cut an oval slightly larger than the dish. Lift this on to the pie dish and press down the edges with your fingers (dip them in cold water first). Decorate the top as you like. Leave a hole for the steam to escape, and brush with a glaze made from the egg and milk. (The chef cuts out leaves and rosettes from the remains of the pastry and decorates the top of the pie with these. He also makes a rosette to cover the hole, which he cooks separately and places over the hole before serving.) Cook the pie in a hot oven, 220 °C (425 °F)/Mark 7, for 10 minutes, then reduce to 180 °C (350 °F)/Mark 4 for 45–50 minutes. Serve with whipped cream or grated Cheddar cheese.

Note: When making several pies, or if you wish to cook in advance, bake the apple pie covered but without the crust for 40 minutes at 190 °C (375 °F)/Mark 5. Cook it again, with the pie crust on before serving, first at 220 °C (425 °F)/Mark 7 for 10 minutes, then at 190 °C (375 °F)/Mark 5 for 15 minutes.

Tarte de Mademoiselle Tatin
Mademoiselle Tatin's Tart

This is my favourite French tart. There are various different ways of making it but I find the chef's recipe one of the best, as it has lots of apple, very little pastry and the caramel is delicious.

SERVES 6–8
100 g (3½ oz) butter
400 g (14 oz) castor sugar
2 kg (4½ lb) cooking apples
300 g (10 oz) shortcrust pastry
   (page 177)

1 tatin mould or a 25-cm (10-in)
   round deep oven dish
silver foil

Coat the mould with the butter. Scatter the sugar over all the buttered mould. Peel the apples, quarter and core them and arrange over the bottom of the mould as if they were petals of a flower. (The top of your mould will then be pretty when you unmould.) Continue to place layers of apple in this way until the mould is full. Cover with a piece of foil paper and place in a moderate oven, 190 °C (375 °F)/Mark 5. The cooking time varies depending on the type of apple and the amount of juice they hold. It should be between 1½ and 2 hours. Halfway through the cooking time, remove the foil paper. When correctly cooked the apples should be a golden caramel colour. Allow to cool a little.

Meanwhile, roll out the pastry very very thinly (about 5 mm (⅕ in) thick, and cut a round 27.5 cm (11 in) in diameter. Leave it to rest for 15 minutes, then cook it for 20 minutes in a moderate oven, 200 °C (400 °F)/Mark 6. When it is cooked, trim it so that it fits the mould. Place the pastry round over the mould. Warm up the mould on the cooking ring, so that the caramel melts slightly. Place a chopping board on top, quickly turn over, and unmould. Cut the tatin into slices. The chef cuts his slices first with scissors and then with a knife as he finds it neater and easier. Arrange on a slightly warmed serving dish. The tart should be tepid, not hot.

Tartelettes au Golden Syrup
Treacle Tarts

Our village baker, Hitchins Bakery in Kintbury, Berks, makes the best treacle tarts in the world. He uses a very old recipe and I once tried to get it from him. But he works on a very large scale and in a very original way. For instance, the recipe began, 'Take a pound of water'. . . . After trying out various recipes this is the one we use. The result is a very good Anglo-French affair which is beautifully made by our pastry cook, Gérard.

MAKES 8
400 g (14 oz) shortcrust pastry
  (page 178)
3 rounded dessertspoons fresh
  breadcrumbs
150 g (5 oz) golden syrup
juice and zest of ½ lemon

8 7.5-cm (3-in) tart tins
1 mixing bowl

Roll out the pastry, cut and use to line the tart tins. (You can, of course, make one tart if you wish.) Leave in a cool place.

Mix the breadcrumbs, golden syrup, lemon juice and zest in a bowl. Spoon this mixture into the tarts. Cut strips of pastry and arrange criss-cross across the tarts. Place the tarts in a moderate oven, 200 °C (400 °F)/Mark 6, for 35–40 minutes. Then turn down to a very cool oven, 110 °C (225 °F)/Mark ¼, until the tarts are cooked. Serve warm.

Crêpes au Gingembre
Ginger Pancakes

This is a light and easy dessert. I think it is safe to say that it was my invention and, like most of the dishes the chef and I adapt, it looks more complicated than it is.

SERVES 8
24 pancakes (page 179)
150 g (5 oz) almonds, sliced
120 g (4 oz) castor sugar
40 g (1½ oz) stem ginger
juice of 1 lemon

1 baking tray
1 mixing bowl

Fold the pancakes in two and cut them into large strips about 2-cm (¾-in) wide. Bake the almonds in the oven until they are golden. Lightly mix the pancake strips, the sugar, (use icing sugar if you prefer), the ginger, the almonds and the lemon juice. Serve warm in a warmed deep serving dish with a hot ginger sauce (page 131).

Meringues Cardinales
Cardinal Meringues

This is a light and pretty dessert which can, and should, be prepared in advance. It is an ideal sweet to serve in the summer. At the Embassy when we serve the delicate little mounds of pink and white meringues they almost match the bowls of roses on the table – and the effect is beautiful.

SERVES 10
whites of 2 eggs
125 g (4½ oz) icing sugar
150 ml (¼ pint) fresh cream
200 g (7 oz) fresh almonds,
  skinned
500 g (1 lb raspberries)
100 g (3½ oz) castor sugar
juice of 1 lemon

1 mixing bowl
1 mixer or whisk
1 spatula
1 icing bag, or small spoon
baking trays
1 liquidizer
1 fine sieve

Beat the egg whites until stiff but not dry. The chef prefers to do this in a copper bowl, using a balloon whisk. You can use a mixer, but be careful not to overbeat. When the whites are stiff, sift the icing sugar over them and gradually fold it in with a spatula. Fill an icing bag with this mixture, or use a small spoon, and arrange about 100 very small mounds on lightly-buttered and floured baking trays. These little mounds should be roughly 2.5-cm (1-in) in diameter. Dry them out in a very cool preheated oven 100 °C (225 °F)/Mark ¼ for 10–15 minutes and then turn the oven off and leave them for at least 5–6 hours in the closed oven.

To serve, beat the cream, spread it between two shells and press them lightly together. Repeat until you have filled the 50 meringues. The chef arranges the little meringues one on top of the other in layers until he obtains a kind of pyramid effect. He decorates the dish with fresh almonds and pours over a little fruit sauce.

The fruit sauce is made by mixing the raspberries and the castor sugar, blending the mixture in the liquidizer and finally pressing it through a fine sieve. Add the lemon juice to the pulp. Serve the rest of the sauce separately in a sauceboat.

Trifle de Cambridge
Cambridge Trifle

This is an adaptation of a traditional eighteenth-century Cambridge recipe. We once served it for a grand buffet we gave for a Scottish party and our French guests were enthusiastic. The chef was a little quizzical and insisted on making it at the very last minute so that it should not be soggy. The result was quite excellent.

SERVES 10–12
For the jelly:
peel of 4 oranges
2 dessertspoons sherry
juice of 4 oranges
juice of 1 lemon
250 g (½ lb) sugar
60 g (2 oz) powdered gelatine

1 mixing bowl
1 heavy pan

For the sponge:
18 macaroons
12 sponge fingers
24 ratafia biscuits
900 ml (1½ pints) fresh cream, beaten
250 g (½ lb) fresh raspberries or raspberry jam
250 g (½ lb) redcurrants or redcurrant jelly
150 ml (¼ pint) Drambuie
juice of 1 orange
juice of 1 lemon
90 g (3 oz) castor sugar

1 deep bowl to serve
1 mixing bowl
1 whisk

To make the jelly, thinly slice the orange peel and leave to macerate for at least 1 hour in the sherry. Then mix the fruit juices with the sherry and add the sugar and the gelatine. (If using leaf gelatine, soak it in cold water first.) Heat gently, stirring all the time, until the sugar and gelatine have dissolved. This should make about 1 litre (2 pints) jelly.

Pour the jelly into a deep glass bowl. When the jelly is beginning to harden, add half the macaroons, half the sponge fingers (cut in three) and half the ratafias. Mix into the jelly. Add 300 ml (½ pint) of the beaten cream and arrange little mounds of the raspberries and redcurrants (or jam) in this cream. (If you are using fresh fruit, toss it first in 2 dessertspoons castor sugar.) Soak the remainder of the macaroons, sponge fingers and ratafias in the Drambuie and arrange them over the mixture. Then beat the remaining cream with the orange and lemon juice and the castor sugar. Add this to the bowl. The cream should come well above the rim of the bowl. Decorate with blanched almonds or pistachio nuts and crystallized fruits.

Coeur à la Crème
Cream Heart

This is a romantic and pretty dish. It is not difficult to do and can be attempted by busy housewives for either a small dinner or – with several hearts – for a buffet. The chef likes to serve a raspberry sauce with it and decorates his plate with some praliné almonds. He likes to keep his 'heart' white but you can, if you prefer, pour some of the sauce over before serving.

SERVES 8

200 g (7 oz) fresh cream (double cream in Britain)

400 g (14 oz) white cream cheese, well drained

400 g (14 oz) raspberries or strawberries

100 g (3½ oz) castor sugar

1 heart-shaped cream cheese mould 20 cm (8 in) in diameter

kitchen muslin

1 plate

1 liquidizer

1 fine sieve

Note: This dish does require a special heart-shaped mould known in France as *un moule à coeur*. These can be bought in Britain, too.

The day before your party line the mould with a piece of kitchen muslin. Beat the cream, mix it with the cream cheese and fill the mould. Place in the refrigerator. The white cream cheese is bound to have some excess liquid in it, so it is advisable to place the mould, which has a perforated base, on a plate in the refrigerator so as to catch the liquid.

Blend the soft fruit and the sugar in a liquidizer and then put it through a fine sieve. Leave this pulp in the refrigerator for a few hours so that the sauce sets. When you wish to serve the dessert, unmould the cheese on to a serving dish, pour some of the fruit sauce round the heart, decorate with praliné almonds (page 182) if you wish, and serve the rest of the fruit separately.

Mousse d'Avocats
Avocado Mousse

The chef serves this in 'homemade' sugar bowls with fluted edges (page 204) and decorates these with green royal icing leaves (page 183). Whatever you serve it in this mousse is very original and we always have fun asking our guests what they think it is.

SERVES 8

25 g (1 oz) pistachio nuts
6 ripe avocados
150 g (5½ oz) castor sugar
juice of 1 lemon
200 g (7 oz) fresh cream

1 saucepan
1 stainless steel sieve
1 mixing bowl
1 glass bowl to serve

Drop the pistachio nuts in boiling water to remove their skins. Cut avocados in half. Scrape out the pulp and put it through a fine sieve. Put the pulp into a bowl and mix in the sugar and lemon juice. Then add the stiffly-beaten cream. Spoon the mousse into a glass bowl and decorate if you wish by drawing lines across with a fork. Scatter the chopped pistachio nuts over the dish and serve.

The mousse is easy to make and should be made as late as possible – just a few hours before serving. The dish should be cold but not iced as it would lose its flavour.

Note: It is advisable to use only stainless steel and plastic utensils for the avocado mousse as this prevents discoloration.

Mont Blanc

This was our favourite dessert when we were children, visiting our relations in Greece. There are, of course, various ways of serving this classic chestnut dish. The one we use in Paris turns out a delicate chestnut mountain, topped with cream (for snow) and surrounded with spun sugar (for the clouds). You may have to do without the 'clouds' as this complicated procedure has to be done not mòre than an hour before the dish is served. When I was just married and tried this dish myself I did not know about the timing and made my sweet in the afternoon and put it in a cool place. When I went to fetch the dish in the evening, hoping it would be a great success and surprise, the sugar had flopped and stuck to my 'mountain'. It was a disaster!

SERVES 6
1 kg (2 lb) chestnuts
600 ml (1 pint) milk
300 g (10 oz) castor sugar
½ teaspoon vanilla essence or
   powdered vanilla
175 g (6 oz) butter, melted
250 ml (scant ½ pint) fresh cream

1 saucepan
1 sieve or food press
1 fine sieve
1 mixing bowl

Peel the chestnuts and then dip them into boiling water for 1 minute or so to be able to skin them. Cook the chestnuts in the milk, sugar and vanilla. Simmer gently for about 40 minutes, and then put through a sieve or food press into a bowl. Add the melted butter. Mix and put through a fine sieve on to a serving dish. (Putting it through the fine sieve makes it very light.) Beat the cream slightly and pour it over the top of your chestnut 'mountain'. You can decorate your dish with *marrons glacés* or spun sugar (page 182). Serve with a chocolate sauce (page 129).

Note: You can press your chestnuts through a fine sieve into a conical strainer and then upturn this on your serving plate – this gives you a mountain peak too. Whatever method you use it is essential not to press down the chestnuts as this makes them heavy.

Lemon Posset

One of the most colourful and delicious lunches for President Giscard d'Estaing during his state visit to Britain in June 1976 was the lunch offered by the Lord Mayor Sir Lindsay Ring at the Guildhall. Sir Lindsay is an expert caterer and gourmet and although it is difficult to serve a large number of guests he managed it to perfection. The menu was:

Sea trout with tarragon sauce
Roast English lamb with damson cheese and mint sauce
New buttered potatoes and broad beans
Raspberries with Cornish cream

All very English and all very fresh. When I congratulated Sir Lindsay on his choice of menu and the manner in which it was served, I asked him if he had any original ideas for English desserts as I liked to serve them in Paris. He immediately said: 'What about Lemon Posset?' and gave me the recipe below, which comes from an old English cookery book published in 1614. We served it in Paris and our guests loved it. It is easy to make and can be made in advance which makes it an excellent sweet for all occasions.

SERVES 8
170 g (6 oz) almond macaroons
850 ml (1½ pints) fresh cream
zest and juice of 2 lemons
170 g (6 oz) castor sugar
2 dessertspoons kirsch
6 ratafia biscuits for decoration

1 glass dish to serve
1 heavy-bottomed pan

Crush the macaroons into a glass dish. Boil the cream with the zest of the lemons. After the mixture has boiled, remove from the heat and add the sugar. Stir well and put aside to cool. Strain the lemon juice and add the kirsch. Add this to the cold cream mixture, pour it over the macaroons, and allow to set. Decorate with ratafia biscuits. The sweet should be made the day before serving and kept in the refrigerator.

Milord Sucre en Visite.

The English 'Milord Sugar'

RECETTES BASES

MASTER RECIPES

Soft-boiled Eggs	Œufs Mollets
Scrambled Eggs	Œufs Brouillés
Poached Eggs	Œufs Pochés
Jellied Meat Stock	Gelée de Viande
Jellied Fish Stock	Gelée de Poisson
Vegetable Stock for Cooking Fish or Shellfish	Court Bouillon
Puff Pastry	Feuilletage
Rough Puff Pastry or Flaky Pastry	Feuilletage Rapide
Pastry for a Pâté	Pâte à Pâté
Sweet Shortcrust Pastry for Tarts	Pâte Sableuse pour Tartes
Shortcrust Pastry for Tarts	Pâte Brisée pour Tartes
Brioche Dough	Pâte à Brioche Maigre
Sponge Cake	Génoise
Pancakes	Crêpes
Sugar	Le Sucre
Spun Sugar	Sucre File
Praliné Almonds	Amandes Pralinées
Royal Icing	Glace Royale
Soft White Icing	Glace Blanche (meringuée)
Quick Chocolate and Coffee Icings and Chocolate Caraque	Glaces au Chocolat et au Café Simples
Butter Filling	Crème au Beurre
Nanny's Butter Icing	Crème de Beurre de Nanny
Italian Meringue	Meringue Italienne
Custard	Crème Anglaise
Basic Custard for Vanilla Ice Cream	Crème Anglaise pour Glace

Oeufs Mollets
Soft-boiled Eggs

6 eggs

1 pan of boiling water
1 pan of cold, slightly salted
  water
kitchen cloth or paper

Cook the eggs in a pan of boiling water for 6 minutes (from the time the water boils *after* the eggs have been put in). Then plunge them into cold water and remove the shells. Keep them in cold, slightly salted water until needed, then drain on a cloth or paper.

Oeufs Brouillés
Scrambled Eggs

1 dessertspoon butter
8 eggs
3 dessertspoons fresh cream
salt and pepper

1 saucepan
1 double boiler
1 egg whisk

Dissolve the butter in a saucepan, break the eggs into it and add the cream, salt and pepper. Place the saucepan in a larger pan containing boiling water. Beat with an egg whisk or wooden spoon until the eggs are cooked. The eggs must not be dry – they must be light; if by any chance they are dry, add another yolk or a little more cream.

Oeufs Pochés
Poached Eggs

12 eggs
vinegar

1 saucepan of boiling water

Have a pan of boiling water ready and add some vinegar (about 2 dessertspoons to 1 litre (2 pints) water). If you will be using the eggs immediately, add 7 g (1 teaspoon) salt for every 1 litre (2 pints) water.

Break the eggs, one at a time, into a cup and slide them gently into the boiling water. Allow them to boil for 3

minutes. The white film must be just solid enough to cover the yolk as the poached egg is, in fact, just a boiled egg without a shell.

Either use the eggs immediately or plunge them into cold water, trim them if necessary and keep them ready in a bowl of cold salted water (about 7 g (1 teaspoon) salt for every 1 litre (2 pints) water) until needed.

The success of a poached egg depends on its freshness – the fresher it is, the lighter and better the poached egg.

Gelée de Viande
Jellied Meat Stock

1 calf's foot
500 g (1 lb 2 oz) veal knuckles, cracked
100 g (3½ oz) pork rind
1 leek, chopped
1 carrot, chopped
1 *bouquet garni* (thyme, parsley, bayleaf)
salt and pepper
whites of 2 eggs

1 large pan
1 cheesecloth

Place the calf's foot, the veal knuckles and the pork rind in a pan of 2.5 litres (4¼ pints) cold water. Bring to the boil and simmer for 5 minutes. Skim, and add 2 cups of cold water to cool. Return the pan to the fire and bring to the boil. Skim, and add the leek, carrot and *bouquet garni*, salt and pepper. Simmer for 3 hours. Strain, and when cold add the egg whites, lightly beaten (this is the clarifying process). Heat gently and stir until boiling point is reached. Then stand the pan off the fire in a warm place for 20 minutes. Finally, pour the stock through a cheesecloth, then place in refrigerator to chill. This makes 2 litres (3½ pints) jellied stock.

Sometimes, and particularly in summer, you may have to add 3–4 leaves of gelatine (15 g (½ oz) powdered gelatine) if the stock is not solid enough. This should be done during the clarifying process.

Note: Jellied stock, ordinary stock and concentrated stock can be frozen and kept until required. Any bones, a chicken carcass and giblets and a little meat with the vegetables used above will make a stock. If you want it concentrated, boil it down after you have skimmed off all the rising scum. Cooking should be gentle – just simmer. Taste before storing to be sure that you have the concentrated taste. (Be careful about adding salt before you boil down for concentrated stock, as you may then find it too salty.) Stock is used for sauces, for deglazing and for pies, etc. You can, of course, use canned bouillon or cubes.

Gelée de Poisson
Jellied Fish Stock

200 g (7 oz) fish bones
300 g (10 oz) firm fish
1 onion, sliced
1 *bouquet garni*
1 clove
500 ml (scant pint) white wine
3 peppercorns
whites of 2 eggs, lightly beaten
10 leaves gelatine

1 large pan
2 clean cheesecloths

Place the fish bones, fish, onion, *bouquet garni*, clove, 500 ml (scant pint) water, the white wine and the peppercorns in a pan and boil for 25 minutes. Strain through a cheesecloth, allow to cool and then incorporate the egg whites and the gelatine leaves. (These should be soaked in cold water for a few minutes before using; you can, however, use 50 g (scant 2 oz) powdered gelatine instead.) Heat up again and bring to the boil, stirring gently. Allow stock to cool for about 15 minutes, and pour through a clean cheesecloth. Chill in refrigerator until cold. This makes 1 litre (1¾ pints) jellied fish stock.

Court Bouillon
Vegetable Stock

1 carrot, sliced
1 medium-sized onion, chopped
2 shallots, chopped
1 *bouquet garni* (thyme, parsley, bayleaf)
250 ml (scant ½ pint) white wine
salt and pepper

1 large pan
1 strainer

Simmer all the ingredients in 2 litres (3½ pints) water for 20 minutes and strain.

This is a stock to use when cooking fish or shellfish. The quantities given here make about 2 litres (3½ pints) stock.

Feuilletage
Puff Pastry

When making puff pastry it is quite a good idea to make more than you need and keep what is left over in the freezer.

500 g (1 lb) flour, sifted
12 g (2 teaspoons) salt
500 ml (scant ½ pint) cold water
1 teaspoon lemon juice
approx. 400 g (1 lb 3 oz) unsalted
   butter

1 mixing bowl or pastry board
1 kitchen cloth
1 marble slab

Sift the flour and salt into a bowl or on to a pastry board. Make a well in the centre and add the water and lemon juice, mixing with a knife or your finger tips. Knead lightly and quickly. Roll the dough into a ball, sprinkle with flour, cover with a cloth and leave in the refrigerator for 20 minutes. Weigh the dough and take half its weight in butter. Knead the butter firm but not too hard. It should have the same consistency as the dough.

Roll out the dough in a square about 20 × 20 cm (8 × 8 in), and about 1.5 cm (½ in) thick. Place the butter in the centre of the dough and fold over to enclose the butter, bringing the sides to the centre. Put this in the refrigerator for 20 minutes. Lightly flour a pastry board or marble slab and, with the joined edge of the dough upwards, place it on the board and roll it out into a strip 60 cm (24 in) long. Fold into 3 with open edges towards you and roll out into another strip (rolling away from yourself). Fold into 3 again and turn, rolling out this time in the opposite direction, with open edges to the left and right of you (see diagram). Repeat the rolling out, folding, turning and rolling 6 times in all, allowing the pastry to rest for 20 minutes in the refrigerator after every second turn. After the final rest of 20 minutes the dough is ready for use or, if wrapped in foil paper, can be kept in a freezer. Cook at 220 °C (425 °F)/Mark 7. This makes about 1.3 kg (2½ lb) pastry.

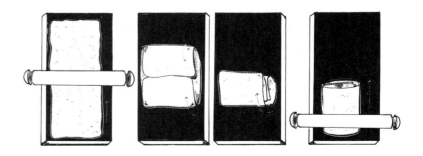

Feuilletage Rapide
Rough Puff Pastry or Flaky Pastry

500 g (1 lb) flour
¼ teaspoon salt
600 g (1 lb 5 oz) butter, not too firm
juice of 1 lemon

1 mixing bowl or pastry board
1 clean cloth

Sieve the flour and salt together into a bowl or on to a pastry board. Make a well in the centre and add the butter, 2 dessertspoons cold water and the lemon juice. Mix rapidly, knead and roll out into an oblong. Fold into 3, half turn the dough bringing the open edges towards you, roll out and fold, turn and roll out again. Turn 4 times in all. Cover with a clean cloth and keep in a cool place for 10–15 minutes. Use immediately. This makes about 1.3 kg (2½ lb) pastry.

Another, more complicated method, but one which produces an excellent light pastry, requires equal amounts of firm cold butter and firm cold lard or margarine. Take 300 g (10½ oz) of each fat and divide into four portions. Cut up into small pieces the size of a walnut. Sieve 500 g (1 lb) flour and ¼ teaspoon salt together into a bowl or on to a pastry board. Make a well in the centre and add the knobs of one portion of the butter, 2 dessertspoons cold water and the juice of 1 lemon. Mix and knead into a firm dough. Roll out into an oblong and scatter over this the knobs of one portion of the cold lard. Fold into 3, turn and roll. Then scatter the remaining pieces of butter, fold, turn and roll. Scatter the remaining pieces of lard, fold, turn and roll. Give another turn and roll. Leave dough in refrigerator for at least 10 minutes before using. The folding and rolling is done as for puff pastry (page 175).

Pâte à Pâté
Pastry for a Pâté

300 g (10½ oz) flour, sifted
pinch salt
80 g (2¾ oz) butter
80 g (2¾ oz) lard
yolks of 2 eggs

1 mixing bowl or pastry board
1 clean cloth

Sift the flour with the salt into a mixing bowl or on to a pastry board. Make a well in the centre and add the butter, lard, eggs and 200 ml (⅓ pint) warm water. Knead to obtain a firm dough, roll into a ball, wrap in a clean cloth and leave in a cool place for 1 hour. This makes about 730 g (1 lb 10 oz) pastry.

Pâte Sableuse pour Tartes
Sweet Shortcrust Pastry for Tarts

120 g (4 oz) fresh butter
80 g (2¾ oz) icing sugar
250 g (9 oz) flour, sifted
pinch powdered vanilla
yolk of 1 egg

1 mixing bowl
1 clean cloth or foil paper

Mix the butter and sugar and then add the flour sifted with the powdered vanilla and the egg yolk and 1 dessertspoon water. Knead, cover and leave in the refrigerator for 3 hours before using. You can keep the dough wrapped in foil in the refrigerator for several days if you wish. Makes about 500 g (1 lb) dough.

Pâte Brisée pour Tartes
Shortcrust Pastry for Tarts

250 g (9 oz) flour, sifted
pinch salt
150 g (5 oz) butter
15 g (½ oz) icing or castor sugar

1 mixing bowl or pastry board
1 clean cloth

Sift the flour and salt together into a bowl or on to a pastry board. Make a well in the centre and put the butter, sugar and 200 ml (⅓ pint) water in this. Mix very rapidly with the tips of your fingers. Knead lightly and form a ball with the soft dough. Wrap it in a cloth and leave in a cool place for about 1 hour. Makes about 600 g (1 lb 5 oz) pastry.

This is the pastry the chef uses in France. In England and the US shortening is added. You may like to use 1 part shortening to 3 parts butter. For savoury tarts and pies omit sugar and add ¼ teaspoon salt.

Pâte à Brioche Maigre
Brioche Dough

7 g (⅓ oz) fresh yeast
250 g (9 oz) flour
2 eggs
100 ml (7 dessertspoons) warm milk
7 g (1 heaped teaspoon salt)
100 mg (3½ oz) butter, softened

1 warm bowl (rinse it in warm water)
1 larger bowl
1 clean cloth
foil paper

Prepare the yeast by diluting it in a warm bowl with 1 dessert-spoon warm water until it is frothy. Add a quarter of the flour. Mix well and form into a ball. Leave it in the bowl, covered with a cloth and in a warm place, to ferment and rise. It should double its volume. Sift the remainder of the flour into a mixing bowl. Make a well in the centre and add the eggs and the tepid milk and mix rapidly. Turn out on to a floured board or kitchen table and knead and slap rapidly until dough is elastic. Stretch dough out and add the diluted salt (dissolve it in a little tepid water), softened butter and the yeast. Mix well, re-form into a ball and leave to rise for 4 hours in a bowl covered with a cloth. Deflate the dough, flatten it out well in the bowl, re-form into a ball and leave in the refrigerator covered with foil to harden. This makes approximately 600 g (1 lb 5 oz) dough.

Génoise
Sponge Cake

SERVES 6–8
4 eggs
100 g (3½ oz) castor sugar
100 g (3½ oz) flour, sifted
100 g (3½ oz) fresh butter

1 electric mixer (or bowl and
  whisk)
1 pan of hot water for *bain-marie*
1 20-cm (8-in) cake tin

Beat the eggs with the sugar in a mixing bowl, then stand the bowl in a pan of hot water over a low heat for about 10 minutes, stirring from time to time, until the mixture is warm. Remove from the pan and beat mixture at high speed until it is cool. Sprinkle in the flour and mix in the lightly melted and cooled butter, using a spatula. Lightly grease and flour the cake tin and pour in the mixture. Place in a preheated moderate oven, 200 °C (400 °F)/Mark 6, for 35 minutes. Unmould on to a cake rack and allow to cool.

Note: If you are using the sponge cake as a base for ice cream, use *half* the recipe.

Crêpes
Pancakes

MAKES 16 THIN PANCAKES
125 g (4 oz) flour
2 eggs
200 ml (⅓ pint) milk
pinch salt
30 g (1 oz) butter, melted

1 mixing bowl
1 fine strainer
1 heavy frying pan

Place the flour in a bowl, add the eggs, cold milk and salt. Mix well and put through a fine strainer. The batter should be light and clear. Add the melted butter and allow the mixture to stand for 3 hours. The batter can be prepared in advance.

The chef uses a pancake pan with a base of 15 cm (6 in) in diameter, and an outside rim of 20 cm (8 in) in diameter. He spoons the mixture into the pan to lightly coat the base and cooks the *crêpes* over a hot plate rather than a flame. He keeps them warm by wrapping them in foil and leaving them in a low oven with the door open, or any warm place.

If you make the pancakes in advance and then fill them later, they must be reheated before serving.

Le Sucre
Sugar

If you frequently make sorbets, sweets, marmalades and jams, you should buy a sugar thermometer and a *pèse-sirop* or saccharometer. The thermometer measures temperature and the saccharometer density. You increase density by boiling the liquid and reducing it; you decrease the density by adding water. A saccharometer or *pèse-sirop* is used for lower temperatures. It measures from 0°–50° density, and is particularly useful when making sorbets. A general guide for these is that 1 kg (2 lbs) sugar to 500 ml (scant pint) water yields 1.1 litres (2 pints) liquid syrup at 32°density.

When it is boiled, sugar changes rapidly from one stage to the next and there is no means of returning it to its previous stage. I have, therefore, listed the various points it reaches from what is known as the 'short thread' to the 'caramel', so that you can recognize them as you cook syrup.

The temperatures listed in the table below show Centigrade and Fahrenheit degrees as marked on a sugar thermometer; degrees of density as marked on a *pèse-sirop*.

	°C	°F	°Density
Short thread	102.6°	215°	25°
Long thread	104°	219°	30°
Small pearl	104.5°	220°	33°
Large pearl	106°	222°	35°
Soufflé (blow)	110°	230°	37°
Feather (or large soufflé)	111°	232°	38°
Small ball	111°–116°	232°–240°	39°
Large ball	119°–122°	246°–252°	40°
Light crack	129°–143°	264°–289°	
Large crack	168°	334°	
Caramel	180°	356°	

If you have no thermometer this is a rough way of judging the different stages, based on stirring, dissolving and then boiling 1 kg (2 lb) sugar in 500 ml (scant pint) water.

1ST STAGE	*Thread* For light syrup	Dip your finger and thumb in a glass of cold water, then dip in the syrup and again in the cold water. Press finger and thumb together and then draw apart slowly. A fine thread of sugar is formed. A larger, stronger thread is formed when the large thread stage is reached. If you do not like the idea of dipping your fingers in the hot syrup, dip a spoon in it, lift it out and when the syrup on the spoon is cool it should drop from the spoon, spinning a small thread.
2ND AND 3RD STAGES	*Pearl* For ices and thick syrups	Large bubbles cover the surface of the pan. If you dip a spoon in the syrup and lift it out, the sugar will drop when cool, spinning a thread at the end of which hangs a bubble of syrup.
4TH AND 5TH STAGES	*Soufflé* For jams etc.	If you twist a wire into a loop and dip it in the syrup and then blow through it, bubbles appear on the other side of the loop. This is the first soufflé stage. As the next one is reached, the bubbles fly about like feathers.
6TH AND 7TH STAGES	*Ball* For fondant and icings	Drop a little syrup into a cup of cold water. After a minute or so roll the sugar in your fingers and it should form a soft ball. For the 'large ball', it should be hard.
8TH AND 9TH STAGES	*Crack* For glacé fruits, etc.	Drop a little syrup into a cup of cold water. When cold it should be hard and break, but if tested between the teeth it should be sticky. Large crack is reached when the tested syrup is hard but does not stick to the teeth. Another method is to drop the hot syrup into a cup of cold water. If the threads of syrup are hard but do not break, the first stage is reached; if they snap easily the second stage has been reached.
10TH STAGE	*Caramel*	When it reaches this stage, the sugar begins to go brown. Remove pan from the heat and plunge it into cold water to avoid further boiling.

Important points when cooking syrup are:

1   Always use a large, clean pan, as syrup rises when it is cooking.
2   Always dissolve the sugar first over a moderate heat, stirring from time to time. When all the sugar has dissolved, remove the scum, cover the pan and boil rapidly until the required stage is reached. Do not stir.
3   The addition of a few drops of lemon juice, a little glucose or cream of tartar is necessary when boiling syrup to prevent crystals forming.

Sucre File
Spun Sugar

This sugar must be used within 1 hour of cooking.

250 g (9 oz) granulated sugar
200 ml (⅓ pint) water

1 heavy pan
2 oiled spatulas
3 large forks
kitchen paper

Boil the sugar with the water to large crack stage (page 181). The chef then proceeds as follows. He takes two wooden, oiled spatulas, traps them firmly in the kitchen drawer and places kitchen paper on the floor underneath them. He lets the sugar cool until it is thick and then dips three forks (which he holds in one hand) into the sugar and raises his hand as high in the air as possible. He passes the forks to and fro over the spatulas very rapidly until all the sugar has been spun on to them. He then carefully removes the spun sugar from the spatulas and places it round the dish he wishes to decorate. For best results the kitchen should be warm and dry, as humidity makes the sugar flop.

Note: You can pass the forks over an oiled rolling pin if necessary, holding it over the paper. The chef tells me that some housewives used to use oiled broom handles.

Amandes Pralinées
Praliné Almonds

250 g (½ lb) sliced almonds
100 g (3½ oz) granulated sugar
whites of 2 eggs

1 baking tin

Mix all the ingredients well and lay out on the baking tin. Place in a preheated moderate oven, 200 °C (400 °F)/Mark 6. Stir and turn the almonds from time to time with a spatula so as to obtain a uniform colouring.

Glace Royale
Royal Icing

whites of 3 eggs
750 g (1½ lbs) icing sugar
juice of 1 lemon
2 teaspoons glycerine (optional)

1 electric mixer, or bowl and
   whisk

If using a whisk beat the egg whites a little until frothy and then beat in the sugar gradually, adding a little of the lemon juice every now and then until all sugar has been added. If using glycerine (which will give the icing a glaze), add it now, then continue to beat until icing is very white and forms peaks.

If you are using a mixer put half the sugar into the mixing bowl with the egg whites and switch on. When well mixed, add the rest of the sugar with the lemon juice and beat until very white and peaks form.

If you cannot use icing immediately, cover bowl with a damp cloth.

Use a drop of food colouring as required. This makes enough to ice one large cake.

Glace Blanche (Meringuée)
Soft White Icing

This is an American recipe but we serve it with an Austrian pudding (page 155). You can of course use it to ice a chocolate cake.

240 g (8½ oz) castor sugar
pinch salt
½ teaspoon cream of tartar or
   lemon juice
1 dessertspoon golden syrup
   (optional)
white of 1 egg, slightly beaten
1 teaspoon vanilla essence or rum

1 medium-sized saucepan
1 mixing bowl
1 mixer or whisk

Put the sugar in a saucepan with 6 dessertspoons hot water, the salt, cream of tartar and golden syrup and cook until bubbles gather round the edge. Then pour over the beaten egg white and continue beating until stiff. Add vanilla or rum and serve or use for cake decoration.

Glaces au Chocolat et au Café Simples
Quick Chocolate and Coffee Icings

This is a water icing or a liqueur icing.

250 g (½ lb) icing sugar
4 rounded dessertspoons grated
  chocolate, or 5 teaspoons
  instant coffee
2 teaspoons vanilla essence
1 teaspoon oil

1 pan with lip
1 double boiler

Put the icing sugar, the chocolate or coffee (dissolve coffee first in 2 dessertspoons hot water), the vanilla essence and 4 dessertspoons water or a liqueur of your choice in a pan (preferably one with a lip to make pouring easier). Place the pan in a double boiler or *bain-marie* over boiling water. Stir and sprinkle in the oil, which will make the icing shine. Stir as the icing is heating up. It should be lukewarm and like a thick cream. Add water if necessary, and when it is ready, pour the icing over the cake. This icing must be used immediately.

Here is another easy way to ice a chocolate cake.

300 g (11 oz) chocolate
100 g (3½ oz) fresh cream

1 double boiler
1 palette knife

Heat the chocolate and cream in a double boiler or *bain-marie* until the mixture is just lukewarm. Stir and spread over cake with a palette knife. You may want to decorate further with chocolate caraque (*copeaux de chocolat*). If you do, place them on the cake before it dries.

For the caraque:
200 g (7 oz) good quality
  chocolate

1 double boiler
1 marble slab or greaseproof
  paper
1 palette knife

Caraque or copeaux:
Melt the chocolate in a double boiler or *bain-marie*. Pour this lukewarm melted chocolate on to a marble slab. When cool, shave it off with a palette knife. Place the caraque pieces in the icing before it dries. If you do not have a marble slab, pour the chocolate over 2 sheets of greaseproof paper and break it into flakes with your fingers.

Crème au Beurre
Butter Filling

This mixture of custard and butter is the chef's recipe and it makes 650 g (1 lb 7 oz) butter icing or filling. When he makes the children's cake – the Coloured Tower (page 200) – he makes 2.5 kg (5½ lb) filling and colours the various layers.

yolks of 5 eggs
125 g (4 oz) castor sugar
250 ml (scant ½ pint) boiling milk
190 g (6½ oz) fresh butter

1 mixer or bowl and whisk
1 heavy pan or double boiler
1 fine strainer

Beat the yolks and the sugar until the mixture is light, then pour in the boiling milk and transfer to a double boiler or to a heavy pan on low heat. Stir and heat gently until the mixture thickens and coats the back of a spoon. Do not boil. Strain through a fine strainer and leave to cool, stirring from time to time to prevent a skin from forming. Beat the butter in a mixer until it is white and light, then pour in the custard slowly, beating all the time. The custard should not be cold but just tepid. Beat and use.

Crème de Beurre de Nanny
Nanny's Butter Icing

This is an easier method of making butter icing, which I have used for all children's birthday cakes. It makes enough for 2 layers of icing or filling on a cake measuring 22 cm (8½ in) in diameter.

120 g (4 oz) butter
225 g (8 oz) icing sugar
yolks of 2 eggs
2 dessertspoons liquid (see method)

1 mixer or bowl and whisk

Beat the butter until soft and light. Beat the sugar and the egg yolks and when these are well beaten add the soft butter and beat again. Finally add the liquid and colouring and beat again.

If using a mixer, start with the soft butter, egg yolks, and half the sugar. Beat well and then add the remainder of the sugar and the liquid and beat at high speed for 5 minutes.

The liquid can be rum, sherry or vanilla essence and a few drops of colouring, or you can make any of the following:

Coffee flavour: Dilute 4 rounded teaspoons instant coffee in 2 dessertspoons water.

Orange flavour: Add the grated rind of 1 orange and a little orange juice (about 1 dessertspoon).

Lemon flavour: Use the grated rind of 1 lemon and 1 dessertspoon lemon juice.

Meringue Italienne
Italian Meringue

This recipe is sometimes called a Swiss meringue. It is used for sorbets, meringues, vacherins, petits fours, etc. You can add your choice of flavours and colours to the basic ingredients.

white of 1 egg
60 g (2 oz) castor sugar
flavouring and vegetable
   colouring (optional)

1 mixing bowl, preferably
   copper
1 balloon whisk
1 pan large enough to hold bowl
   (for *bain-marie*)
baking tins

Mix the sugar and the egg white in a bowl. Stand the bowl in a pan of hot water over a low heat and beat with a whisk until the warmed mixture is stiff and sticks to the wires of the whisk.

To make meringues, arrange little mounds of the egg and sugar mixture (after you have added the flavouring and vegetable colouring) on buttered and floured baking tins. Bake in a preheated very low oven 110 °C (225 °F)/Mark ¼ for 10–15 minutes. Then turn the oven off and leave to dry out for 4–5 hours.

For sorbets, use the meringue uncooked and add to sorbet mixture when it has thickened. It makes the ice lighter.

Crème Anglaise
Custard

yolks of 5 eggs
125 g (4 oz) sugar
250 ml (scant ½ pint) milk

1 mixer or bowl and whisk
1 heavy pan
1 strainer

Cream the egg yolks and sugar well (I do this in a mixer). Boil the milk and pour immediately over the yolks and sugar, return to the pan and heat until boiling point, stirring continuously. Strain and allow to cool, stirring from time to time to prevent a skin forming on surface. This makes 350 ml (12 fl oz) custard.

Crème Anglaise pour Glace
Basic Custard for Vanilla Ice Cream

SERVES 8
½ vanilla pod
750 ml (1½ pints) milk
yolks of 10 eggs
200 g (7 oz) castor sugar
100 g (3½ oz) fresh cream, beaten

1 large heavy-bottomed pan
1 large mixing bowl
1 strainer
1 ice cream churn

Heat the vanilla and milk together. Beat the egg yolks and sugar in a mixing bowl until they are frothy and white. When the milk boils, remove the pan from the heat and add the egg and sugar mixture, stirring all the time. Return the pan to the heat and stir until the mixture coats the back of the spoon. Do not allow to boil, as this would make it curdle. Strain through a fine strainer and allow to cool, stirring from time to time to prevent a skin from forming. Pour into an ice cream churn and churn until almost ready, then add the beaten cream and churn again.

Punch English-style, the recipe for which includes four barrels of brandy, 25,000 limes, 80 pints of lemon juice and 2,300 kilogrammes of sugar

DIVERS

MISCELLANEOUS

FOR COCKTAIL PARTIES	**POUR LE COCKTAIL**
Small cheese tarts for cocktail parties	Tartes au Fromage pour cocktail
Welsh Rarebit for cocktails	Welsh Rarebit pour cocktail
Chicken and curry mince pies	Mince pies de poulet au curry
Vienna Crackers	Biscuits de Vienne
SUMMER TEA	**LE THÉ D'ÉTÉ**
Iced tea	Le thé glacé
Watercress or cucumber sandwiches	Sandwich au cresson ou concombre
Toasted bacon and tomato sandwiches	Sandwiches toastés au bacon et à la tomate
SUMMER DRINK	**BOL D'ÉTÉ**
Giovanni's Sangria	Sangria Giovanni
WINTER PUNCH	**PUNCH D'HIVER**
Hot spiced wine	Vin chaud aux épices
CAKES FOR TEA	**LES GÂTEAUX POUR LE THÉ**
Plum cake	Plum cake
The chef's chocolate cake	Gâteau au chocolat du chef
Scones	Scones
FOR CHILDREN	**POUR LES ENFANTS**
Coloured tower for children's parties	Tour colorée pour les enfants
Iced petits fours	Petits fours glacés
FOR CHRISTMAS, WEDDINGS AND BIRTHDAYS	**POUR NOËL, LES MARIAGES ET LES ANNIVERSAIRES**
Christmas, wedding and birthday cake	Gâteau de Noël et d'anniversaire
CHEF'S SPECIALITY	**SPECIALITÉ DU CHEF**
Sugar bowls	Coupes en sucre
Almond icing	Pâte d'Amandes
FINALE	**FINALE**
Hendersons' Favourite Dish: Pear Tart	Tarte aux Poires

Tartes au Fromage pour Cocktail
Small Cheese Tarts for Cocktail Parties

You can make the tart shells in advance, keep them in a box and fill them with the cheese mixture when needed. We use the very small moulds and the following mixture makes about 50 tarts, 3.5-cm (1½-in) in diameter.

400 g (14 oz) shortcrust pastry
   (page 178)
100 g (3½ oz) butter
60 g (2 oz) flour
400 ml (14 oz) fresh cream,
   slightly heated
7 eggs
250 g (½ lb) Gruyère or Cheddar
   cheese, grated
salt and freshly-ground black
   pepper
1 teaspoon French mustard

Grease the tiny tart moulds and line them with pastry. Make a béchamel (page 121) with the butter, flour and cream. Add the eggs, beating them in one by one, then the cheese, salt, pepper and mustard. Fill the tart moulds and place them in a preheated moderate oven, 200 °C (400 °F)/Mark 6, for 15 minutes.

Welsh Rarebit pour Cocktail
Welsh Rarebit for Cocktails

We like to serve very small Welsh rarebits for our cocktail parties, and the chef has found an original way of making his toast. Here is the recipe and method we use.

Welsh rarebit mixture (page 24)
white bread

2 pastry cutters, one 5 cm (2 in)
   and one 2.5 cm (1 in)
1 pointed knife
1 baking tray

Approximately 500 ml (scant pint) Welsh rarebit mixture makes 80 rounds.

Slice your bread about 1 cm (½ in) thick and cut out rounds about 5 cm (2 in) in diameter with a pastry cutter. Cut smaller rounds inside them (but only halfway through the bread) with a 2.5-cm (1-in) cutter. Toast the rounds either under the grill or in the oven. Using a pointed knife, carefully remove the little lid formed by the small cutter. Fill the hollow with a teaspoonful of Welsh rarebit mixture. Place the filled rounds on a baking tray and bake for 3–4 minutes in a preheated moderate oven, 200 °C (400 °F)/Mark 6. Serve hot.

Mince Pies de Poulet au Curry
Chicken and Curry Mince Pies

This is the 'house's' invention or adaptation. We serve it for cocktails and press conferences. It makes a change from the more usual cheese tarts.

MAKES 20

300 g (10 oz) pie dough (page 178)
½ chicken, cooked
150 ml (¼ pint) béchamel (page 121)
2 dessertspoons currants (optional)
salt and pepper
1 dessertspoon curry powder

20 little tart tins (ours are 3.5 cm (1½ in) in diameter)
1 mixing bowl
baking tins

Line the little tart tins with the dough and allow them to stand while you prepare the filling.

Dice the chicken meat, chop it into very small pieces and add it to the béchamel. Mix in the currants, salt and pepper to taste and add the curry powder. Fill the shells. Wet the sides of them with a little water and cover with 'lids' cut out of the remaining dough. Press these down and prick them. Allow them to stand for a while, then arrange them in baking tins and bake in a preheated moderate oven, 200 °C (400 °F)/Mark 6 for 15–20 minutes. Cool a little and unmould. We serve these pies warm in a dish lined with a napkin which we fold over the top of the pies to keep them warm.

Biscuits de Vienne
Vienna Crackers

These were our favourite salted crackers when we were in Vienna. I tried to work out the recipe, having bought them at that famous cake shop, Demmels. We now make quite a lot of them and keep them to offer when people come to drinks. We also serve them at cocktail parties.

200 g (7 oz) puff pastry (page 175)
yolks of 2 eggs
2 teaspoons milk
1½ dessertspoons poppy seeds
1½ dessertspoons caraway seeds

1 baking sheet
1 pastry brush

Roll out the pastry in a rectangle 40 × 30 cm (16 × 12 in). It will be about 2 mm ($\frac{1}{16}$ in) thick. Place this on a greased pastry baking sheet, brush over with a glaze made from the egg yolks and milk and prick the pastry with a fork to prevent it rising. Scatter the poppy seeds over half the pastry and the caraway seeds over the other half. Put the pastry in the refrigerator for 10 minutes so as to make cutting easier. Remove from the refrigerator and cut in diagonal strips or squares. If you cut the strips into squares 3 × 3 cm (1¼ × 1¼ in) you will have some 70 crackers. Allow the pastry to stand for 10 minutes after you have cut it. Then place in a moderate oven, 200 °C (400 °F)/Mark 6, for 3 minutes. Take them out and press down with the base of a clean heavy pan, tin or something similar. Return to the oven for 3–4 minutes to dry out. Serve warm, piled into a little round bowl.

These crackers can be made in advance and heated when you wish to serve them. You can scatter sliced almonds, pistachio nuts or salt instead of the poppy seeds and caraway.

Le Thé Glacé
Iced Tea

This is a perfect summer drink, even if you cannot enjoy it in a beautiful Embassy garden. It tastes just as good wherever you are on a hot summer's day.

FOR ABOUT 8 PEOPLE
1 pot strong tea
juice of 4–6 lemons
rind of 1 lemon
rind of 1 orange
1 cucumber, sliced and peeled
large sprig mint
115 g (4 oz) sugar
750 ml (1½ pints) ginger beer

1 tea pot
1 sharp knife
1 glass or earthenware jug

Use Indian or China tea, or a mixture of both, depending on your taste. We use Twinings' Earl Grey. Carefully make about 1 litre (2 pints) tea. Use 1 teaspoon tea per person, heat the pot first, and be sure the water is boiling when you pour it into the heated pot.

Put the lemon juice (I use 6 lemons), lemon and orange rinds, cucumber slices and rind, mint and sugar in a jug. Try to cut the rinds and peel all in one piece, like a snake; they are best that way. Pour over the hot tea and stir. When cold, add the ginger beer and keep in refrigerator until ready to serve. Serve iced in glasses.

You can alter the recipe according to your taste, using orange and lemon slices, cherries, more or less sugar, but the above recipe is the one we prefer.

Sandwich au Cresson
Watercress Sandwiches

4 large slices white bread (see method)
250 g (9 oz) soft white cheese, drained
100 g (3½ oz) fresh butter, softened
1 dessertspoon Colman's mustard
salt, pepper and paprika
2 bunches watercress

1 mixing bowl
greaseproof paper
kitchen cloth

The bread slices should be cut from a large, long loaf, and measure 40 × 15 cm (16 × 6 in). They should be about 2.5 mm (⅛ in) thick.

Mix the cheese, butter, mustard, salt, pepper and paprika together, then add the watercress and mix lightly. Use only the leaves of the watercress. Place a sheet of greaseproof paper on a kitchen cloth (the kitchen cloth is optional but keeps the process clean and helps with the rolling up).

Lie 2 slices of bread on the paper, one in front of the other with the long side facing you. (The two slices together should form a rectangle of about 40 × 30 cm (16 × 12 in) – one slice on its own is not big enough to roll up.) Spread half the cheese and watercress mixture over the slices and roll up as for a Swiss roll. You will find it easier to roll up if you use the greaseproof paper and cloth to flip the bread over and over. When you have rolled the bread up, wrap tightly in the sheet of paper and leave in the refrigerator for at least 3 hours. Repeat the procedure on a clean piece of greaseproof paper with the other 2 slices of bread and the other half of the filling.

After 3 hours, unwrap the rolls and cut them into slices. Arrange in a serving dish over a napkin and decorate with a bunch of watercress.

For cucumber sandwiches, take 2 large cucumbers, peel, remove pips, slice in thin *julienne* and scatter salt over them so as to remove excess liquid. Mix with the cheese, etc as mentioned above and proceed as for watercress sandwiches.

Sandwiches Toastés au Bacon et à la Tomate

Toasted Bacon and Tomato Sandwiches

SERVES 8

4 large tomatoes
16 slices white bread, about 1 cm
   ($\frac{1}{2}$ in) thick
150 g (5 oz) butter, softened
juice of 1 lemon
pinch of salt and pepper
6 lettuce leaves, sliced in strips
16 slices bacon, crisply fried

1 pan for tomatoes
kitchen paper
1 sharp knife
1 wire rack
1 heavy weight

I have never tasted such delicious sandwiches as the ones the chef serves. They are tiny, fresh and irresistible. He serves them before the theatre or some official function, when guests will be unable to have dinner until later in the evening.

Skin the tomatoes by dropping them in boiling water for a few seconds. Then slice them, remove the pips, and leave the slices to dry out on absorbent kitchen paper.

Toast both sides of the bread and use a very sharp knife to cut each slice in half through the middle (this leaves you with one toasted side and one untoasted side). Lay out 16 of these half slices with the untoasted side up. (Keep the other 16 slices on one side.) Mix the butter with the lemon juice and salt and pepper. Butter the slices of toast and arrange the lettuce strips on them, then the thin tomato slices, then the bacon (crushed into small pieces) and finally cover with the 16 other half slices of toast. Place a wire rack over them and put a heavy weight on top to flatten them. Before serving cut off the crusts and divide each sandwich into 4. Serve on a white napkin (the chef likes lace ones) and decorate with a bunch of watercress.

Sangria Giovanni
Giovanni's Sangria

SERVES 10

3 litres (5 pints) red wine
1.5 litres (2½ pints) Perrier water
4 oranges, sliced and quartered
1 lemon, sliced and quartered
3 peaches, diced
2 apples, diced
500 g (1 lb) castor sugar
50 ml (3½ dessertspoons) gin
100 ml (7 dessertspoons) whisky

1 large earthenware bowl with
  cover

This is the Italian butler's recipe which we serve for summer buffets and parties in the garden. My daughter Alexandra once served it in London at a party she gave in Dorset Square. She prepared bowls and bowls of this sangria and she was particularly delighted that it could be made in advance, as she had to rush home from work to serve her friends. I gather the party was a huge success – the sangria had to be topped up because it was running out, but no one noticed the difference.

Pour the wine and Perrier water into a large earthenware bowl and then add the fruit and the sugar. Stir, and add the gin and whisky. Mix and leave in the covered bowl in the refrigerator for 24 hours. Serve chilled in glasses.

Vin Chaud aux Épices
Hot Spiced Wine

SERVES 6–8

5 dessertspoons Cognac
140 g (5 oz) granulated sugar
1 level teaspoon cinnamon
4 large slices lemon
4 cloves
150 ml (¼ pint) water
1 litre (2 pints) red wine

1 large heavy pan
1 strainer
1 jug

A good winter drink for a party on a cold night. We serve it at Christmas parties. You can use any inexpensive red wine you wish.

Bring all the ingredients except the wine to the boil. Simmer for 5 minutes, then add the wine and heat again. The mixture must be hot but not boiling. Strain into a warm jug, preferably earthenware or china, and serve in glasses. To make more, increase quantities in proportion.

Plum Cake

This is a cake we always have ready to serve to guests for tea. It keeps well and is what the French call le plum cake. It is a combination of my Dundee cake recipe and the chef's recipe for a plum cake.

250 g (9 oz) fresh butter
100 g (3½ oz) castor sugar
5 eggs
1 teaspoon baking powder
1 teaspoon mixed spices
300 g (10 oz) flour, sifted
350 g (12 oz) candied fruits, diced and mixed
3 dessertspoons rum or brandy
50 g (1¾ oz) almonds, skinned and split

1 mixer, or bowl and whisk
1 spatula
1 deep cake tin with removable base, 16 cm (6½ in) in diameter

Beat the butter and sugar in an electric mixer until light and white. Add the eggs one by one, beating all the time. Sift the baking powder and mixed spices with the flour. Mix the candied fruits into the flour. Add this mixture to the other ingredients very gradually, beating and mixing all the time. Finally add the rum or brandy. Turn out into the buttered and lightly-floured cake tin and bake in a moderate oven, 190 °C (370 °F)/Mark 5, for 1 hour. Leave to cool in the tin. If you are not using the cake immediately, unmould and keep wrapped in silver foil. You can decorate the cake by arranging some split almonds on the top before baking.

Note: For a traditional Dundee cake you can add 150 g (5½ oz) mixed currants and sultanas.

Gâteau au Chocolat du Chef
The Chef's Chocolate Cake

This is the chef's adaptation of the famous Austrian Sachertorte recipe which I gave him. We serve it for tea parties and sometimes, split in half and filled with whipped cream, for buffets. The traditional Austrian cake can be split in half with apricot jam in the middle as well as under the chocolate icing.

150 g (generous 5 oz) fresh butter
160 g (scant 6 oz) granulated
  sugar
8 eggs
180 g (6½ oz) chocolate
100 g (3½ oz) flour
1 teaspoon baking powder
50 g (1¾ oz) potato flour
50 g (1¾ oz) powdered almonds
200 g (7 oz) sieved apricot jam
3 dessertspoons rum or liqueur

1 mixer or bowl and whisk
1 *bain-marie*
1 cake tin with removable rim,
  30 cm (12 in) in diameter
1 small pan

Beat together the butter and sugar until light. Add the eggs one by one, beating all the time. Break up the chocolate and melt it in a *bain-marie*, then add to the mixture and beat well. Add the flour and baking powder sifted together, the potato flour and powdered almonds, and beat again. Turn out into a lightly greased and floured cake tin and cook for 1 hour in a preheated moderately slow oven, 170 °C (325 °F)/Mark 3. Leave to cool, and then unmould on to a wire cake rack.

Mix the apricot jam with the rum or liqueur in a small pan, heat, and leave to simmer until it has reduced its volume by about one-third. It should be thick enough to coat the back of a spoon. Strain, pour over the cake top and allow to cool.

Cover the cake with royal icing (page 183), white icing (page 183), or fondant icing, for which you will need 400 g (14 oz) fondant sugar heated together with 150 g (5 oz) melted chocolate to 36°–37° on the saccharometer. Add water if necessary so that you can pour icing over cake rapidly.

If you are using white icing or beaten cream it is a good idea to decorate the cake with chocolate caraque (page 184).

Scones

We serve scones instead of bread for our lunches and dinners. They are always fresh and warm and greatly appreciated by our French guests. We serve them in silver bowls covered with starched napkins to keep them warm.

MAKES 20
500 g (1 lb 2 oz) flour, sifted
1 dessertspoon baking powder
¾ dessertspoon salt
200 g (7 oz) fresh butter
250 ml (scant ½ pint) milk
yolk of 1 egg
2 dessertspoons milk

1 mixing bowl
1 crinkled cutter
1 pastry brush
1 baking tray

Sift the flour, baking powder and salt into a bowl and quickly mix with the butter and milk. The exact quantity of milk depends on the quality and type of flour: you should aim at a soft dough. Knead very lightly and roll out the dough to a thickness of about 2.5 cm (1 in). Cut with a round crinkled cutter. Brush over with a glaze made from the egg yolk and extra milk and bake in a moderate oven, 200 °C (400 °F)/Mark 6, for 15 minutes. Serve warm.

Tour Colorée pour les Enfants
Coloured Tower for Children's Parties

This idea came to me when I was making birthday cakes for my daughter. I started off by adding another layer to her cake every year. Of course when she was no longer a child I gave this up, and now she has the traditional iced fruit cake (page 202). It is, however, amusing to have lots of layers with coloured soft icing in between and children love cutting this giant cake.

5 20-cm (8-in) *génoises* or sponge cakes (page 179)
2.6 kg (5½ lb) soft butter icing (page 185)
vegetable colouring and flavours

4 mixing basins
1 *bain-marie*
1 whisk or mixer
1 cake base or cardboard round and foil paper

Divide your butter icing into 4 equal parts and place them in different mixing basins. Colour and flavour them individually (this is easier if the icing is warmed slightly over a *bain-marie*), and then beat with a whisk or in a mixer. The following are some of the colourings and flavours we use:

> *Green*: Add a little vegetable colouring and pistachio essence.
> *Coffee*: Use a little instant coffee.
> *Pink*: Add a little vegetable colouring and strawberry essence.
> *Chocolate*: Add a little cocoa powder.
> *Orange*: Use a little vegetable colouring and orange essence.

Have your cake base ready. If you do not have one, cut one out in cardboard and cover with foil. Place the first *génoise* in the centre and start building your tower with layers of *génoise* and layers of butter icing in different colours in between. When you have laid the last layer of *génoise* it is a good idea to put the cake in the refrigerator for the butter icing to harden. Then you can take it out and decorate as you wish with white icing, royal icing or chocolate icing and chocolate shavings, etc. At one Christmas party the chef covered it with different coloured icings in the shape of a Napoleonic drum. The drum sticks were made out of sugar. (For icings see pages 183–4.)

Petits Fours Glacés
Iced Petits Fours

You can make these with coffee, chocolate or any flavour and vegetable colouring you wish by adapting the recipe below. We serve these little cakes for children's parties; they are small, light and pretty. We find, on the whole, that children prefer grilled sausages, nuts and potato crisps to heavy cream cakes. These petits fours *are just small enough and amusing enough to be tempting. There are never any left over.*

MAKES 20–25

1 *génoise* using 4 eggs (page 179)
rum
250 g (½ lb) butter filling (page 185)
500 g (1 lb) fondant sugar
flavouring and vegetable colouring (vanilla, coffee, rum, etc)

1 rectangular Swiss roll or similar cake tin, 15×30 cm (6×12 in)
1 cake rack
1 heavy pan for fondant
1 wooden spoon

Bake the *génoise*. Allow to cool and then cut in half through the middle. Sprinkle a little rum over the two pieces. Spread the butter filling over one piece and cover it with the other. Cut into small squares about 3 cm (1¼ in) square. Place these in the refrigerator to allow the butter icing to harden. Then arrange on a cake rack (laid over a shallow pan), leaving a space between each *petit four*. Heat the fondant sugar in a small heavy pan and stir with a wooden spoon. Add the flavour of your choice and the colouring, and a little water or syrup if the fondant is too hard. It should be at body temperature: if it's too cold it is difficult to spread; if it's too hot it will not have a shiny texture.

Ice each little cake by taking a spoonful of the fondant and pouring it slowly over the centre of the cake, letting it drip and cover the sides. You can collect any of the fondant which falls into the pan, reheat it and use it again. Decorate the top with sugared violets or pistachio nuts, etc.

Note: You can use any of the quick icings (page 184) instead of the fondant, and substitute apricot glaze for the butter filling. To make this, heat 250 ml (½ pint) sieved apricot jam with 3 dessertspoons liqueur.

Gâteau de Noël et d'Anniversaire
Christmas, Wedding and Birthday Cake

The chef has become a real birthday-cake expert. He decorates the traditional British fruit cake with royal icing, coloured candles (25 for the Silver Jubilee Dinner and 60 for Yehudi Menuhin's birthday), and sugar figures. We use this recipe for wedding, christening and Christmas cakes too, varying the decoration.

MAKES A LARGE CAKE 27 CM
(11 IN) IN DIAMETER

500 g (1 lb) butter or margarine
350 g (12 oz) brown sugar
4 eggs
2 teaspoons baking powder
½ teaspoon ground mace
1 teaspoon powdered cinnamon
500 g (1 lb) flour
1 kg (2 lb) mixed currants,
    sultanas and raisins
250 g (½ lb) mixed candied peel,
    chopped
250 g (½ lb) almonds or walnuts,
    chopped
1 teaspoon vanilla essence
150 ml (¼ pint) rum
5 dessertspoons milk
4 dessertspoons brandy or rum

1 mixer or bowl and whisk
1 sieve
1 deep cake tin with removable
    rim, 27 cm (11 in) in diameter

Beat the butter or margarine and sugar until white and light, then add the eggs, one at a time, beating well. If you like, mix the sugars: 2 parts brown to 1 part castor. Sieve the baking powder and spices with the flour and add to the butter mixture alternately with the mixed fruit, peel and nuts (i.e. 2 dessertspoons flour mixture, then 2 fruit, etc). Beat well each time you add the fruit and each time you add the flour. Finally add the vanilla, rum and milk. Beat again as you incorporate these.

Grease the cake tin and line it with greaseproof paper or foil. If the tin is shallow, tie a collar of lightly-greased paper round it to prevent the mixture spilling over. Pour the batter into the tin and bake in a slow oven, 150 °C (300 °F)/Mark 2, for 4–4½ hours, covering after the first hour with two layers of greaseproof paper or foil. After 4–4½ hours switch off heat and allow the cake to cool in the oven.

Unmould, and sprinkle with a little brandy or more rum. When cold, wrap in foil paper and keep until required.

Note: This cake is better made in advance and even better if it is moistened with a light rum or brandy syrup. My cook in Berlin, Mrs Knor, would make her Christmas cakes well in advance and wrap them up in foil paper. A little later, but while the cakes were still warm, she would pour over a syrup made with 250 ml (scant ½ pint) water, 3 dessertspoons sugar and 2 dessertspoons brandy or rum. Then she would wrap the cakes up again. She would do this about 4 or 5 times before icing the cakes. You can do this, too, when the cake is already cut and you wish to keep it fresh. Just turn it over gently and pour a little syrup over the bottom of the cake. It makes the cake easier to cut and keeps it fresh and delicious.

Traditionally the rich fruit cake is covered with almond icing and royal icing (page 183).

Pâte d'Amandes
Almond Icing

250 g (½ lb) ground almonds
250 g (½ lb) icing sugar
250 g (½ lb) castor sugar
1 teaspoon vanilla essence
1 large egg or 2 small ones
1½ dessertspoons lemon juice

1 mixer, or bowl and wooden
   spatula or spoon
1 pastry board
greaseproof paper (optional)

Put all the ingredients in an electric mixer and switch on. If you do not have a beater, use a wooden spatula or spoon to mix the almonds with the icing and castor sugar in a bowl. Add the vanilla and the eggs and mix well. Finally add the lemon juice.

When the ingredients are well mixed you should have a firm paste. Roll this out on a board lightly dusted with icing sugar, or between two pieces of greaseproof paper dusted with icing sugar. Cut to fit cake. It is easier to roll out the icing larger than the cake, lift it over the cake and let the icing hang down over the sides, then trim to fit and press down the edges. This makes enough to ice one large cake.

Coupes en Sucre
Sugar Bowls

These are so pretty and so impressive that they are worth attempting for a special occasion. This is the chef's method.

1 kg (2 lb) sugar
400 ml (⅔ pint) water

1 heavy pan with lid
1 marble slab or baking tray
1 palette knife
2 salad bowls

Cook the sugar in the water until it has reached the caramel stage (page 180). Pour it over a lightly-oiled marble slab or oiled and warmed flat baking tray so that you have two rounds (that is if you want one large and one small bowl – one for the ice and the other for biscuits, cream or almond balls which will accompany your ice or cream.) The large bowl needs a round about 30 cm (12 in) in diameter; the smaller one should be 20 cm (8 in) in diameter. Unstick the rounds with a palette knife and press them over the upturned, lightly-oiled salad bowls. You can pull the sugar bowls out and shape them as you wish while the sugar is warm. Allow to cool, and then unmould. You can decorate the edges of these bowls with coloured royal icing (page 183). If you have fluted salad bowls the shape is prettier.

Tarte aux Poires
Pear Tart

Finally there is nothing so French as a pear tart – Tart aux Poires. It is our favourite dessert – Nicko, my husband, Alexandra and Derry Moore, my daughter and her husband, and all our English guests love it. So here it is, as made by the chef, a simple but delicious grand finale.

SERVES 6
4 firm large pears, peeled
syrup (see method)

For the frangipane:
50 g (1¾ oz) castor sugar
50 g (1¾ oz) butter
2 eggs
50 g (1¾ oz) ground almonds

300 g (10 oz) shortcrust pastry
   (page 178)

1 saucepan
1 mixing bowl and whisk, or
   mixer
1 25-cm (10-in) tart ring
1 forcing bag

The pears should be of excellent quality. Poach them in the syrup made with 1 litre (2 pints) water to 250 g (½ lb) sugar. The cooking time depends on the quality of the pears; they should be firm. Drain, cool, halve and core carefully, then thinly slice each quarter across very carefully without disturbing the shape.

Make a *frangipane* by beating the sugar and butter well, then adding the eggs one by one and finally beating in the ground almonds.

Carefully roll out the pastry on a lightly-floured surface and line the ring or tart tin. Pipe (using a bag if you wish) or lightly spread a little *frangipane* on the base of the tart. Arrange the pear halves like a star over this and press each half down so that the slices show. Fill the spaces between the pears with *frangipane*. Cook in a preheated oven, 200 °C (400 °F)/Mark 6, for 30 minutes. Serve cold or just warm with a bowl of cream. *Note:* The chef uses rings without bases for his tarts and places these on baking trays. This is an excellent idea as it cooks the base of the tart and makes it crisper but you can, of course, use a tart tin with removable rim if you wish.

Any left over *frangipane* can be used to make *petits fours* by piping little moulds on to a baking tin and cooking them in the oven. These can be served with ice cream or fruit salad.

Recipe Index